Twayne's United States Authors Series

Sylvia E. Bowman, *Editor*

INDIANA UNIVERSITY

Robert Ingersoll

ROBERT INGERSOLL

By DAVID D. ANDERSON
Michigan State University

 204

Twayne Publishers, Inc. : : New York

*To William B. Thomas,
friend for many years*

PREFACE

Robert Green Ingersoll was a man who perhaps could have achieved prominence only in America in the second half of the nineteenth century. A man who thrived on controversy, his prominence was as paradoxical as his nature, and he was unique in his time, even unique, perhaps, in American history. A popular, entertaining, and controversial lecturer in an age that eagerly sought such entertainment, his fame was based not only upon his universally admitted talent and skills but also upon the rational and emotional eloquence with which he regularly denounced the orthodox religious beliefs of his listeners. A humanist who sought and foresaw the coming of a perfect society for man on earth, he was an economic and social conservative who opposed many of the reforms that attempted to hasten the arrival of that society. An ardent and active Republican, he neither sought nor achieved high elective or appointed office during two generations of Republican domination. A champion of the Negro, he was almost silent as second-class citizenship became a reality. A kindly, well-loved man in his friendships, he was bitter and merciless toward his enemies. A rationalist, he did not hesitate to wave the Bloody Shirt in the heat of political campaigns.

The paradox in his nature was equally evident in the attitudes of his comtemporaries toward him. To his friends and his supporters, he was in the grand tradition of literary artists and human liberators, standing, perhaps, just below Shakespeare and Lincoln in the hierarchy of each; to his enemies, particularly among the religious orthodoxy, he was the devil incarnate. Yet many of these same orthodox found in him a sincere friend with much that was admirable in his character, but others found him sarcastic and merciless. Like Thomas Paine and others who became part of the long conflict between rationalism and theology, Ingersoll became almost a legendary figure in his own time, and the myths that emerged at his death threatened to obscure the reality of his talents, his beliefs, and his personality.

Undoubtedly the paradoxes in his nature are partially responsible for the fact that even yet, despite the perspective made possible by the passage of time, the evolution of ideas, and the acceptance of much that was considered heresy in his day, it is difficult to approach

Ingersoll with objectivity. The recent studies and editions of his works are either admittedly or obviously partisan; in some circles, he is still used to frighten children; in others, he is considered a fearless pioneer. My own students find it impossible to read "Why I Am An Agnostic" with either apathy or objectivity. Ingersoll becomes to them a hero or a heretic who is to be accepted or denounced with a lack of critical perception that belies their averred sophistication and open-mindedness.

More important, however, than the paradoxes in Ingersoll's life and beliefs in contributing to the lack of a critical approach to his work and ideas is the fact that Ingersoll is rarely read today except in the transcripts of lectures that give little evidence of his personality or of the range of his ideas as they were reflected in the context of his times. Even more rarely are they seen for what they are: way stations in the evolution of human thought. Almost never are they seen as the products of an active, inquiring, if sometimes naive, mind or as the expression of one of the most eloquent orators in an age of oratory uncorrupted by electronic amplifiers or teleprompters.

The sterotyped interpretations of Ingersoll's works, as they continue to survive, are themselves the product of stereotypes. His father was an orthodox Calvinist minister; therefore, Ingersoll's hostility to religion was the product of youthful rebellion. He was an antislavery Union officer; therefore, he was a Republican. He was a wealthy man; therefore, he was an economic conservative. These stereotypes are likely to endure because of the very nature of the emotional atmosphere that continues to surround the controversies of which he was a part. Unfortunately, as a result, they not only obscure the reality of a complex and interesting man but also distort one of the most exciting chapters of the history of ideas in America, of the nineteenth century, and of the ancient, continuing conflict between rationalism and supernaturalism, between religious orthodoxy and free thought.

Neither a savior nor an Antichrist, Ingersoll was not a profound or original thinker or writer. He was, more than anything else, the spokesman for an age of change—undoubtedly an age that brought about changes more profound than any other in American history. Born in an America torn between fatalistic acceptance of man's perfidy and increasing conviction that he has in him the seeds of perfection and wisdom; maturing in a rapidly disappearing frontier area in which the race went to the swift and able; steeped in the law that was the product of eighteenth-century rationalism and revolution; imbued with the atmosphere of an age of humanistic reform, of romantic concern for one's fellows; and coming to prominence with the new industrialism that made possible great wealth and great poverty, Ingersoll was the product of all of these forces and much more. Perhaps most significantly, he was the product of an age that saw Romanticism destroyed by Darwinism, inhumanity, and the machine and of an age that continued to give lip service to humanistic ideals while seeking a material reality. The paradoxes of the age gave rise to the paradoxes of Robert Ingersoll, just as they gave rise to a curious consistency too often obscured by the paradoxes and by the stereotypes one choses to accept.

This consistency is the consistency inherent in the changes—economic, social, political, intellectual, and scientific—that made the twentieth-century world a reality; and it is this consistency that exists beyond the paradoxes, a unity in spite of apparent diversity that I attempt to make evident in this study. Neither a great writer nor a great thinker, with his undoubted greatness as an orator lost because his gifts were primarily those of immediacy rather than permanence, Ingersoll remains alive for the modern world in the twelve volumes of his collected works, in the countless letters that he wrote, and in the dusty files of both great and obscure newspapers. These are the modern world's intellectual heritage from Robert Ingersoll and it is these upon which this study is based. Certainly they convey little of the power of his presence, and yet they provide a substantial basis for a study that will hopefully achieve objectivity.

This purpose of this study is, then, to approach Ingersoll as thinker and as writer rather than as orator and to determine his contributions to the histories of ideas and of letters. Neither biography nor social history in intent, it will nevertheless be something of both as I attempt to employ whatever critical tools are necessary in order to achieve understanding.

Lansing, Michigan   DAVID D. ANDERSON

ACKNOWLEDGMENTS

For the many kinds of assistance that enabled me to write this book, I am deeply grateful: to the staff of the Michigan State University Library, the State Library of Michigan, and the Lansing Public Library for their many courtesies; to Michigan State University for the research grant that supported the study; to Miss Sylvia E. Bowman for her sympathetic editorial assistance; and again to my wife Pat for her help and encouragement.

CONTENTS

CHRONOLOGY

1833   Robert Green Ingersoll born at Dresden, New York, on August 11.

1839–   Attended school intermittently in Ohio, Wisconsin, and Illinois.
1852

1852–   Taught in subscription schools in Mount Vernon and Metropo-
1854   lis, Illinois, and in Waverly, Tennessee.

1854   Admitted to the Illinois bar in December after reading law in Marion, Illinois.

1855–   Practiced law with his brother Ebon in several Illinois towns.
1861

1860   Gave first anti-theological lecture, "Progress," at Pekin, Illinois; was Democratic candidate for Congress in the Fourth Illinois District; denounced the Fugitive Slave Law in a speech at Galesburg; defeated overwhelmingly.

1861   Mustered into federal service as Colonel, Eleventh Regiment, Illinois Volunteer Cavalry, on December 20.

1862   Married Eva A. Parker on February 13; participated in the battle of Shiloh, April 6 and 7; appointed Chief of Cavalry, Sixth Division, on December 2; captured by General N. B. Forrest's troops on December 17.

1863   Paroled in March; resigned from the service on June 30; returned to Peoria, Illinois, to practice law; became a Republican.

1867–   Appointed and served as attorney general of Illinois; became
1869   active in Illinois Republican politics, speaking in Illinois and later in Indiana, Iowa, and Maine in support of General U. S. Grant for the presidency; supported the Radical Republicans nationally.

1868   Unsuccessfully sought the Republican nomination for the governorship of Illinois.

1869– Became successful corporation and criminal lawyer in Illinois;
1877 began to acquire reputation as orator and agnostic.

1872 Wrote "The Gods."

1873 Wrote "Individuality."

1874 Wrote "Heretics and Heresies."

1876 Was successful in the notorious *Munn* case; became nationally prominent as Republican after nominating James G. Blaine in the Republican national convention; later supported Rutherford B. Hayes for the presidency; wrote "Vision of War."

1877 Wrote "Ghosts" and "The Liberty of Man, Woman, and Child"; moved on to Washington, D. C.

1878 Toured England; wrote "Robert Burns."

1880 Wrote "What Must We Do to be Saved?"; campaigned for James A. Garfield after his nomination for the presidency. Wrote "Some Mistakes of Moses."

1881 Wrote "Some Reasons Why" and "The Great Infidels."

1882– Was successful in the *Star Route* trials resulting from the postal
1883 scandals.

1884 Wrote "Orthodoxy" and "Which Way?"; broke with James G. Blaine.

1885 Wrote "Myth and Miracle"; moved to New York.

1886 Supported Henry George for mayor of New York.

1888 Supported Benjamin Harrison after his nomination for the presidency.

1891 Wrote "Shakespeare" and "Liberty in Literature"; began the famous Davis will case.

1894 Wrote "About the Holy Bible" and "Abraham Lincoln."

1895 Wrote "The Foundations of Faith."

1896 Wrote "Why I Am An Agnostic" and "How to Reform Mankind"; supported William McKinley for President with vigor.

1897 Wrote "The Truth" and "A Thanksgiving Sermon."

1898 Wrote "Superstition."

1899 Wrote "The Devil" and "What Is Religion?"; warned against jingostic imperialism after the Spanish-American War; died on July 21.

Robert Ingersoll

CHAPTER 1

"The great fact of my being . . ."

THE decade of the 1830's was one in which America began to find its identity, its direction, and its voice. In 1820 Andrew Jackson had assumed leadership of the country, and the center of political strength and social, moral, and economic values moved west of the Appalachians, following the path of human migration that insisted that American destiny and freedom lay to the west, along the path of empire. Dynamic, pragmatic, and democratic, optimistic, determined, materialistic, and yet motivated by a paradoxical faith and fatalism, a diverse people sought and began to find an identity as Americans and a direction that demanded progress and insisted upon a goal of perfectibility. Rude, energetic, confident, emotional, and anti-intellectual, the decade of the 1830's was the age of Jackson and of the open society. In that decade the test of the individual was his own talents, and the role of government was to provide opportunity and support for his efforts. The age made an indelible imprint upon the character of the people and upon the events of the century.

Unquestionably the age of the common man and the open society, the age was also one of the individual who sought his own identity and his own voice; and the temper of the times sought to permit him the freedom to find them. Consequently, it was an age of reform that sought consciously to bring about the perfect society and an age of faith in man's ability to do so. The restless dynamism of the West as it sought to build a nation was the spectacular reflection of a more subtle but no less significant movement that sought to articulate and direct man's drive for freedom, for progress, and for faith in his own ability to map out his destiny.

On its lowest levels, the new faith in man manifested itself in a shifting of religious emphasis as acceptance and ultimate salvation became open to all who were determined to follow the path of righteousness. No longer did God determine who was or was not to be saved; the decision was the individual's own as religious orthodoxy reflected the new democratic impulse. The drive toward utopia sought not merely social but individual perfection, and it was manifested in movements to make realities of both. Educational development, prison and penal law reform, and other equally idealistic activities marked the path for the great social reform movements of the century: the women's rights movement, the temperance movement—and above all, eventually dominating, absorbing, and ultimately dissipating the reform energy of a determined people—the Abolition movement that sought to remove a mocking shadow from a society increasingly democratic.

The intellectual apex of the decade was that which sought to give spiritual dignity to man as an extension of rather than as a servant and plaything of his Creator. This movement was that of Transcendentalism, at the heart of which was the belief that man, God, and the universe were one, spiritual, and good. As the decade opened, a young Unitarian minister was pondering his break with theology, beginning his search for a higher ultimate unity, and making notes for an essay designed to give synthesis and articulate meaning to the restless search of his time. At the end of the decade, Transcendentalism was established, as were the role, the identity, and the faith of Ralph Waldo Emerson.

During the decade, horse-drawn streetcars appeared on the streets of New York; Cyrus McCormick's reapers began to be seen on prairie farms; the typecasting machine and vulcanized rubber became realities; and steam-packet service was established on the Transatlantic run. Between 1830 and 1840 the population of the United States increased by one third or by almost five million persons. One of them, born on August 11, 1833, at Dresden, New York, a hamlet scarcely removed from its frontier origins, was Robert Green Ingersoll.[1]

The youngest of five children, three sons and two daughters, born to the Reverend John and Mary Livingston Ingersoll, Robert was heir to the intellectual, social, and theological controversies and conflicts of that tumultuous period as they were epitomized in his own family and environment. The Reverend John Ingersoll was a graduate of Middlebury College, an ordained Congregational minister who also served Presbyterian pulpits, and a devout Calvinist. But his era increasingly rejected the rigidity of Calvin's Five Points in favor of an open salvation reflecting an increasingly open society. Consequently, John Ingersoll was a man of the past, a learned man, a logician, and a conservative in an epoch characterized by non- if not anti-intellectualism, by emotional fervor, and by dynamic change. As American destiny moved west, the Reverend Ingersoll moved his brood with it, seeking a permanence and a role that the age denied him. In spite of his learned eloquence, he was fated to be a wanderer.

Mary Ingersoll died when Robert was two, but her influence over the boy continued beyond her lifetime as the older children, Ruth, born in 1822, John Livingston, born in 1823, Mary Jane (1826), and Ebon Clark (1831) continued to preserve her memory and her ways. Active in the Temperance movement and in the drive to abolish slavery in the District of Columbia, Mary Ingersoll felt little if any of the theological convictions of her husband, even to the extent of reportedly having read and admired Thomas Paine's *The Age of Reason.* But she was firmly dedicated to the cause of social reform and to her family. The Ingersoll home was apparently stern but happy, like so many others of the period, and Mary Ingersoll gave herself to its service and to the harsh demands of small town parsonages. In 1835, at the age of thirty-five, she died at Cazenovia, New York. John Ingersoll did not marry again until seventeen years later.

During those seventeen years, Robert Ingersoll's formative years, the family was very close, dominated by the exhorting fundamentalism of the father, encumbered by comparatively little formal education. Yet the family was characterized by strong affection and loyalty and by a relentless intellectual curiosity as together they followed the calls of Calvinistic pastorates from New York City, where John Ingersoll preached in Charles Grandison Finney's Broadway Tabernacle, to the west. He served in Oberlin, Ashtabula, and other towns in Ohio's Western Reserve and then briefly in Kentucky, Indiana, and Michigan. After an unsuccessful attempt at storekeeping in Wisconsin, he returned to the pulpit in Greenville and Marion in Illinois. The family never prospered, nor did it enjoy security, but it was not impoverished; and, as a church family, it maintained appearances and a firm if sometimes threatened hold on respectability. All of the children were destined to do well in the open society of the West.

As the focal point and strength of the family, John Ingersoll must have been impressive. Although the rigidity of his Calvinistic faith has often been singled out as the source of his youngest son's later iconoclasm, the evidence suggests that such an interpretation is an oversimplification that ignores the profound positive influence of the father on his son. The Calvinistic routine, particularly on Sunday, was oppressive, as Ingersoll later recalled; but he had learned to live with it:

In the olden time they thought some days were too good for a child to enjoy himself. When I was a boy Sunday was considered altogether too holy to be happy in. . . . Nobody said a pleasant word; nobody laughed; nobody smiled; the child that looked the sickest was regarded as the most pious. . . . Then we went to church. The minster was in a pulpit about twenty feet high, with a little sounding board above him, and he commenced at "firstly" and went on and on to about "twenty-thirdly." Then he made a few remarks by way of application; and then took a general view of the subject, and in about two hours reached the last chapter in Revelation. . . . Then came the catechism with the chief end of man. . . . The minister asked us if we knew that we all deserved to go hell, and we all answered "Yes." Then we were asked if we should be willing to go to hell if it was God's will, and every little liar shouted "Yes." Then the same sermon was preached once more, commencing at the other end and going back. After that, we started for home, sad and solemn—overpowered with the wisdom displayed in the scheme of the atonement. When we got home, if we had been good boys, and the weather was warm, sometimes they would take us out to the graveyard to cheer us up a little. It did cheer me. When I looked at the sunken tombs and the leaning stones, and read the half-effaced inscriptions through the moss of silence and forgetfulness, it was a great comfort. The reflection came to my mind that the observance of the Sabbath could not last forever.[2]

If the atmosphere of the Sabbath and the harshness of the doctrines practiced in the Ingersoll home were oppressive, Robert Ingersoll saw neither as the source of his agnosticism. He denied that his father had anything to do with his lack of faith; he insisted that from an early age he simply did not believe in eternal punishment, and from that point he had no faith in the specifics or generalities of orthodox Christianity. Although John Ingersoll believed firmly in the biblical injunction that to spare the rod was to spoil the child and although he was also determined to save his children from a fiery hereafter, Robert Ingersoll insisted, nevertheless, that his father "was a man of great natural tenderness, and loved his children almost to insanity. The little severity he had was produced by his religion."[3]

This attitude toward children, unmitigated by a religious fear that he did not feel, dominated Robert Ingersoll's relations with his own children and also what he conceived to be the proper method of rearing them. It is evident that much of the tenderness that characterized his own family life resulted from the closeness of his motherless home, but it is equally evident that much of the public Robert Ingersoll also was derived from the manners, habits, and persuasions of his father.

John Ingersoll was not merely a Calvinistic clergyman; he was an orator, an Abolitionist, and a Democrat—all of which combined to influence Robert as he approached manhood. John Ingersoll derived much of his revivalistic fire, his antislavery fervor, and his democratic faith from his admiration for Charles Grandison Finney, who had been his Presbyterian mentor and sponsor; and the combination, refined but no less real, was transmitted to his son. An impassioned as well as eloquent preacher, John Ingersoll made his son aware of the potential inherent in skillful oratory; one who denounced slaveholding as sinful, often to the scandal of anti-Abolitionist parishioners, he implanted that conviction in his son; and a man with great faith in the democratic dream of an open and free society, he pointed out Robert's path to prominence and wealth. At the same time, he implanted a sense of duty, of responsibility, and of stewardship that Robert was neither to forsake nor forget—even when he joined forces with the leaders of the Gilded Age.

John Ingersoll provided his son with an education that was as eclectic as it was informal, resulting in the mastery of an impressive and extensive body of knowledge. Himself a Greek, Latin, and Hebrew scholar, as well as a wide reader in the tradition of the New England clergy, John Ingersoll apparently did not insist that his children attend school regularly; and Robert never described his formal educational background. Apparently, he attended grammar schools in Ohio and Wisconsin and briefly attended a subscription school, taught by one Socrates Smith, in the basement of the Congregational church of Greenville, Illinois. At sixteen he wrote verses, one of which, "The Wavy West," was published in the Greenville *Journal.*

During these years, apparently with the encouragement of his father, he read widely, much of which was in the standard Calvinistic classics: Calvin's *Institutes,* Jonathan Edwards' *The Will,* Milton, John Bunyan's *Pilgrim's Progress,* John Foxe's *Book of Martyrs,* and a good many more. But their designed impact, to reinforce the dominance of a Calvinistic faith, had just the opposite effect on young Robert. Like Benjamin Franklin a century before, he rejected orthodoxy partly as a result of inept attempts to support it.

These works and others of the great ages of English prose and poetry did, however, contribute to Ingersoll's awareness of the vividness and power inherent in the English language; and, increasingly, as he turned to nontheological reading, again largely from the seventeenth and eighteenth centuries, he pursued the study of language as well as of ideas, the medium as well as the content, knowing that the two were inseparable from each other and from his own destiny. He read Edward Gibbon, William Cowper, Byron, Keats, Shelley, Voltaire, Thomas

Paine, Volney, and others; but the greatest impact and the greatest revelation came from Shakespeare and Robert Burns. In later years, he often re-created the impact of the discovery of both as they gave him insight into the mind, the heart, the language, and the greatness of man. In 1895, he wrote:

When I went into the shop of the old Scotch shoemaker he was reading a book, and when he took my shoes in hand I took his book, which was "Robert Burns." In a few days I had a copy.... It was in my mind night and day. Burns you know is a little valley, not very wide, but full of sunshine; a little stream runs down making music over the rocks, and children play upon the banks; narrow roads overrun with vines, covered with blossoms, happy children, the hum of bees, and little birds pour out their hearts and enrich the air. That is Burns.... (XII, 172)

If Burns provided Ingersoll with a vision of man's joy, Shakespeare provided one of his glory:

While I was waiting for supper an old man was reading from a book, and among others who were listening was myself. I was filled with wonder. I had never heard anything like it. I was ashamed to ask him what he was reading; I supposed that an intelligent boy ought to know. So I waited, and when the little bell rang for supper I hung back and they went out. I picked up the book; it was Sam Johnson's edition of Shakespeare. The next day I bought a copy for four dollars. My God! more than the national debt.... For days, for nights, for months, for years, I read those books.... Other writers are like a garden diligently planted and watered, but Shakespeare a forest where the oaks and elms toss their branches to the storm, where the pine towers, where the vine bursts into blossom at its foot. That book opened to me a new world, another nature. While Burns was the valley, here was a range of mountains with thousands of such valleys; while Burns was as sweet a star as ever rose into the horizon here was a heaven filled with constellations. That book has been a source of perpetual joy to me from that day to this; and whenever I read Shakespeare—if it ever happens that I fail to find some new beauty, some new presentation of some wonderful truth, or another word that bursts into blossom, I shall make up my mind that my mental faculties are failing.... Those, then, are two things that helped to educate me a little. (XII, 172-73)

In one of Ingersoll's most famous and controversial lectures, "Why I Am An Agnostic," he dwells again on the insight given him by his reading, and he culminates his statement with a comparison that points to Shakespeare as the source of his conviction:

And then I read Shakespeare, the plays, the sonnets, the poems —read all. I beheld a new heaven and a new earth; Shakespeare, who knew the brain and heart of man—the hopes and fears, the loves and hatreds, the vices and virtues of the human race; whose imagination read the tear-blurred records, the blood-stained pages of all the past, and saw falling athwart the outspread scroll the light of hope and love; Shakespeare, who sounded every depth—while on the loftiest peak there fell the shadow of his wings.

I compared the Plays with the "inspired" books—Romeo and Juliet with the Song of Solomon, Lear with Job, and the Sonnets with the Psalms, and I found that Jehovah did not understand the act of speech. I compared Shakespeare's women—his perfect women—with the women of the Bible. I found that Jehovah was not a sculptor, not a painter—not an artist—that he lacked the power that changes clay to flesh—the art, the plastic touch, that moulds the perfect form—the breath that gives it free and joyous life—the genius that creates the faultless.

The sacred books of all the world are worthless dross and common stones compared with Shakespeare's glittering gold and gleaming gems. (IV, 39-40)

If Burns and particularly Shakespeare opened for Ingersoll visions and vistas impossible to find in the narrow Calvinist world of his father, the rationalism of the eighteenth century provided him with the tools of analysis, of critical appraisal of tangible evidence, and of constructing a tenable hypothesis. To Volney, he attributed his rational approach to religious belief; to Gibbon, both the method of gathering evidence and interpreting it as well as the facts of the origins of the Christian religious superstructure. To Voltaire, he attributed his faith in humanism and his hatred of cant and hypocrisy. The rationalism and skepticism of the Neoclassics led inevitably to the Classics—Zeno, Epicurus, Socrates, and Diogenes—who reinforced his growing disbelief and made possible another significant comparison: "I compared Zeno, Epicurus and Socrates, three heathen wretches who had never heard of the Old Testament or the Ten Commandments, with Abraham, Isaac and Jacob, three favorites of Jehovah, and I was depraved enough to think that the Pagans were superior to the Patriarchs—and to Jehovah himself" (IV, 45).

If this eclectic reading provided Ingersoll with the basis for rejecting not only the Calvinism of his father but the entire range of theological conviction, it was Thomas Paine's *Age of Reason* which showed him the basis for the convictions he was to hold for the rest of his life. Paine, he wrote, was "one of the heroes, who gladly gave his life, his every thought and act, to free and civilize mankind" (IV, 43). The freedom of man intellectually and politically remained one of Ingersoll's great dreams, and it drew him inevitably from the Democrat party of his youth into the new Republican party which had came into being as the party of freedom, dedicated to the eradication of slavery. Paine remained his hero—although, he conceded, Paine had not gone far enough in his rejection of religious superstition.

Although Ingersoll's self-education continued for the rest of his life, his omnivorous and yet logical reading habits were ingrained in his philosophy. Reinforced by an innate distrust of a higher educational structure, whether public or private, that was dominated by conventional religious beliefs, he used his own experience as the basis for the later education of his daughters. He entrusted neither of them to a system that, as he insisted, replaced truth with the Bible.

Ingersoll's own formal education ended at Greenville, Illinois, in 1852, when, after the minor achievement of publishing his verse in the local paper, he decided to become a schoolmaster. Certification—approval by a county commissioner after a brief examination—was easy; and for the next two years he taught at Mount Vernon and Metropolis, Illinois, and at Waverly, Tennessee. Although during these years he became imbued with the Abolitionist doctrines of Owen Lovejoy and of his father, who began to preach that dangerous doctrine with religious fervor, Ingersoll, like so many other ambitious boys of the age, turned to law. Of all the things he had ever done, he later stated, teaching school was by far the worst; and he would have no more of it.

Becoming a lawyer was at the time little more difficult than becoming a schoolmaster; and, after returning from Tennessee to Marion, Illinois, he began to read law in the firm of Willis Allen and his son William, prominent Democrats. Willis, the father, had been a congressman, and his son William was to be one in the future. Both were lawyers of ability. At the same time, Robert began to work as assistant clerk of the circuit and county court. On December 20, 1854, together with his brother Ebon Ingersoll, at the age of twenty-one, he became a member of the Illinois bar.

Still Democrats through the slavery controversies of the 1850's, the Ingersoll brothers found their Democratic faith reinforced by the Allens as they entered the practice of law, first in Shawneetown and later in

Peoria, Illinois, in what was the most dynamic legal and political period in that state's history. Not only was the array of lawyer-politicans who dominated the decade of the 1850's impressive—Abraham Lincoln, Stephen Douglas, David Davis were among them—but the state itself was beginning to reflect the coming split in the nation, one that was to affect their law practice, their thinking, and ultimately their personal and political philosophies as well as the course of their lives as it threatened the life of the nation itself.

Both Ingersolls found the atmosphere in Shawneetown, in the Egypt of Illinois, oppressive socially, culturally, and ideologically. An impoverished area settled largely by those who had moved north as they moved west, it was underdeveloped, proslavery, and hopeless. To Robert Ingersoll, it represented an affront to man's dignity, a denial of his hope, and a foreshadowing of his death. In 1857, the Ingersoll brothers moved their law firm to Peoria to be free of the area of Southern influence and enter the mainstream of the movement of people and ideas from New England to the west. Both found the new atmosphere congenial and profitable; but, as true Westerners, they remained faithful to the Democratic party.

While Ebon served a term in the state legislature as a representative from Gallatin County during 1856-57, Robert began to establish a reputation for articulateness, shrewdness, and psychological skill that remained the basis of his legal and public reputation. During the early years in Peoria, Ingersoll, like Lincoln in Springfield a generation before, rose from relative poverty, to prominence and respectability, if not affluence. The law was yet, as it was throughout the nineteenth century, a relatively sure means by which a poor but bright and ambitious boy might ride the crest of the socially mobile times as civilization became secure in the West.

Like other lawyers of the time and place, Ingersoll's practice was varied, including both criminal and civil cases and leading him inevitably toward active, practical political participation. On the circuit from county courthouse to county courthouse, Ingersoll—his later bulk foreshadowed as he passed 180 pounds at twenty-four—rode horseback, accepted cases as they came, and built his reputation and prosperity. By 1860, he had become a leading young Democrat, an orator of local note—he delivered his first antireligious lecture, "Progress," in Pekin, Illinois, in 1860—and he met Eva Amelia Parker, daughter of a prosperous Groveland family of impeccable revolutionary ancestry and also of free-thought leanings. In 1862, while Ingersoll was on active military service, they were married.

In 1860, perhaps the most critical election year in American history, Ingersoll was selected as the Democratic candidate for Congress from the Fourth District, the one surrounding Peoria. On July 4, he gave the local patriotic oration at the town's celebration, a successful event that gave him much personal popularity, and his chances of election appeared to be excellent. His opponent was the much older Republican incumbent, Judge William Kellogg, a man who, in the tradition of Daniel Webster and Abraham Lincoln, professed to be a moderate; he was opposed to slavery but was willing to permit it to continue where it existed, even to the extent of accepting the desirability as well as constitutionality of the Fugitive Slave Law.

Although the campaign in the Fourth District reflected in miniature the nationwide confusion of the confrontation between pro- and antislavery men, most of Illinois' attention was devoted to the campaign as an aspect of the continued conflict between Stephen Douglas and Abraham Lincoln, while John Breckenridge and John Bell, whose candidacies were to decide the issue, were almost totally forgotten. In Peoria and the surrounding area, the campaign—and Judge Kellogg's and Ingersoll's roles in it—was largely an extension of the Lincoln–Douglas debates of 1858.

Kellogg, like Lincoln, insisted that the federal government prevent the extension of slavery into the territories; but Ingersoll replied that the Republicans saw the people in the territories as infants to be bound in congressional-applied diapers. Ingersoll was thereupon called "the Diaper Candidate" by his opponents; but he went on to the attack with such vigor and conviction that, in a speech at Galesburg, he denounced the Fugitive Slave Law—the skeleton that occupied the closets of both parties. Ingersoll had seen the law in operation in southern Illinois; he knew that Lincoln, like Douglas, was willing to live with it; but he himself, unlike his opponent and his own party, could not live with it:

> The Fugitive Slave Law is the most infamous enactment that ever disgraced a statute book. . . . The man who approves of or apologizes for that infamy is a brute! . . .

> Judge Kellogg favors and approves all these horrors. . . . And yet he is no worse than all the trusted leaders of your boasted Republican party. Your Abe Lincoln himself, . . . distinctly declares himself in favor of the enforcement of the Fugitive Slave Law, as do all the Old Line Whigs who made up the warp and woof of the Republican party.[4]

With Lincoln supporters horrified and with Douglas Democrats alienated by such a head-on confrontation with an issue they had hoped to avoid, and with a law which many of them also supported, the outcome was evident at this point, although the campaign continued by moving into the mud-slinging, personally vituperative phase that dominated much of frontier political life. When the returns were in, Judge Kellogg had won easily in the district, as had Lincoln; but Ingersoll had carried Peoria by a slim margin. Ingersoll's first active campaign for political office had been futile and embarrassing.

Nevertheless, the campaign was extremely significant for him. Not only did it focus upon the spark that was to inflame the nation, but it marked Ingersoll's last major appearance as a Democrat as the Civil War and Abolition turned his convictions into Republican allegiance. Quickly becoming a War Democrat, he followed the flag into the army, and he later followed his brother Ebon, who became a War Democratic candidate for Congress, supported by a Republican endorsement, into the Republican party, a political allegiance that was to dominate the rest of his life. As a patroit and a believer in freedom, he could abide no measures that were compromising or incomplete.

On December 20, 1861, after having spent three months raising three regiments of volunteer cavalry, Robert Ingersoll was sworn into federal service as colonel commanding the Eleventh Regiment, Illinois Volunteer Cavalry. His war service was comparatively short but eventful; and, to a great extent, it was responsible for the intensely nationalistic patriotism that colored his political convictions from that time. On February 13, 1862, he married Eva Parker, and a few days later he was ordered to the western war theater. On April 6 and 7, he participated in the battle of Shiloh; and, on December 2, he was appointed Chief of Cavalry of the Sixth Division. But on December 17 he was captured, after a spirited engagement, by troops under the spectacular Confederate General Nathan Bedford Forrest. Paroled in March, as was customary in the early years of the war, Ingersoll reluctantly awaited formal exchange; then, frustrated by the terms of parole, he resigned from the service on June 30.

When Ingersoll returned to Peoria to practice law in the summer of 1863, his intellectual development and his personal and public philosophies were complete. The rest of his life was devoted to the propagation of his convictions on the lecture platform, in the courtroom, and on the campaign trail. Almost immediately after his return, his law practice flourished; and he turned increasingly to corporation law, representing various Illinois railroads. Perhaps as a result of his practice, combined with his own growing affluence and his conviction that, just as he had risen in the socioeconomic hierarchy of America, so could others, he became increasingly conservative economically. Ultimately, both his beliefs and his growing courtroom skill and knowledge of the law led to his participation in many of the celebrated trials of his day, including the notorious *Star Route* scandal trials that lasted throughout much of 1882 and 1883 and the great Telegraph suit of 1887. His growing reputation and practice led him to move from Peoria to Washington, D. C., in late 1877 or early 1878, and finally to New York City in the fall of 1885.

In 1867, largely as a result of his new-found Republican loyalty, Ingersoll was appointed attorney-general of Illinois, and he served until 1869 in a position that brought him close to the political powers in Illinois; and in 1868 he decided to seek the governorship. He was led to believe that he was the first choice for the gubernatorial nomination of a majority of delegates to the Republican State Convention of May 6, 1868, and that Major General John M. Palmer, a powerful and popular Republican leader, would not run. But Palmer did run; and, although Ingersoll fought for the nomination, he was defeated by a ballot of 317 to 117.

During and after the intraparty struggle for the nomination, Ingersoll's unorthodox religious views became an issue both in fact and in legend. Ingersoll had never made a secret of his views; indeed, as in later life, he was inclined to wear them proudly, and they were common knowledge, particularly among party men, throughout the state. Although there is no evidence to suggest that his beliefs played any role in his defeat, and although the evidence indicates that Palmer's success was foregone and Ingersoll's candidacy the result of faulty information or communication, the myth emerged, nevertheless, that the religious question was raised by the convention delegates, that Ingersoll was promised support if he would be sworn to silence about his views, and that he eloquently refused.

Actually, such a confrontation was extremely unlikely. Not only is evidence, other than hearsay newspaper accounts of the alleged meeting, totally lacking; but Ingersoll certainly would not have ignored the incident in citing evidence in later years to display the power of censorship. Furthermore, the confrontation was unnecessary. When Palmer entered the contest, the conclusion was inevitable since delegates repaid the political debts they had accrued with Palmer in the ultimate political coin with which such obligations are paid.

Nevertheless, Ingersoll's unsuccessful bid for the governorship had two major effects: his Republican allegiance did not waver (although it was strained when Rutherford B. Hayes won the nomination over James G. Blaine in 1876), but he determined never again to seek public office. Instead, he determined to devote all his energies to the law and to lecturing in order to support his family, now augmented by two daughters, Eva Robert Ingersoll (born September 22, 1863) and Maud Robert Ingersoll (born October 4, 1864).

When Ingersoll determined to pursue his private vision of success as a lawyer and as an orator rather than in a political career, he was thirty-six years old, secure in his legal reputation, happy in his home life, talented as an orator, and fixed in his personal philosophy. Almost at once he began to formalize, to disseminate, and to exploit his increasingly unorthodox ideas. Possessed of wit, imagination, and rhetorical talent, he was also characterized by a passion for facts, an instinct for the psychological jugular vein of his opponents, and a commanding presence. His manner of delivery, whether in the courtroom or on the lecture platform, was almost cold; he acted as if he had determined not to use the highly charged delivery of his clerical critics. Although he used emotional appeals in both courtroom and lecture hall, he used them for calculated effect, just as he used the logical evidence that he amassed: as a rapier to cut, thrust, parry, and ultimately demolish rather than as a miasma to obscure the issue and to stultify opponents, audience, or jury.

Descriptions of his oratorical techniques and effectiveness abound. In the courtroom or on the lecture platform, he was dramatically and deceptively simple; he shunned props, aids, or distracting influences as he stood alone, seeming to speak spontaneously and impulsively, often with neither notes nor manuscript. Dispensing with traditional introductions, he calmed the audience with a simple dramatic gesture and then began to speak, almost as if in conversation, and yet clearly and forcefully as well as confidentially. Speaking rapidly, using his voice as effectively as a musical instrument, he rejected both the stance and the gestures of the grand declamatory tradition; instead, he used only a few simple gestures, each of which was gracefully and carefully controlled. Rarely, perhaps as a result of nervousness, did he pace back and forth; and on at least one occasion he stubbed his toe as he did so.

Testimonies to his oratorical effectiveness came from supporters and critics, skeptics and orthodox, obscure reporters and famous writers, clergymen, politicans, and industrial giants, many of whom gave further testimony to his personality as they became his friends. Clarence Darrow sought to emulate him; Mark Twain insisted that his command of the language was beyond comparison; Walt Whitman described his delivery as "precious ointment"; Edgar Borah and Albert Beveridge, both of whom pursued successful political careers, studied his techniques; Andrew Carnegie regarded him as a great American man of letters; Henry Ward Beecher insisted that he was the greatest speaker in the English language on earth; and Eugene Debs was so fascinated by a lecture in Terre Haute in 1878 that he followed Ingersoll to Cincinnati. He became Matchless Bob, Handsome Bob, and Royal Bob to friends and opponents alike. He was, without question, the great orator of his day, an age which sought effective oratory avidly, judged it un- equivocally, and surrendered to its spell with abandon.

Perhaps the common factor in the attempts to describe Ingersoll's effectiveness was his sincerty; the depth of which was unquestioned not only by his supporters but by his opponents who heard him speak in spite of their constant assertions that his only interest in his causes was financial. But the evidence of the documents that survive is unmistakable; his sincerity is evident throughout, as are the range, the curious inconsistencies, the paradoxes, and the conviction of truth. As political thinker, humanist, lawyer, agnostic, supporter of the arts and of the good life, he insisted that all could and would be reconciled—that man's hope for freedom and happiness was in his own hands, mind, and heart. In the wide range of his statements, he attempted to point the way.

CHAPTER 2

"The thing called law . . ."

ADMITTED to the bar in Illinois in 1854, Ingersoll practiced the profession for the rest of his life; in the process, he moved from small-town Illinois to New York City, from a rural practice based upon the tedious trivia of frontier legislation to the sophisticated and celebrated cases of rascality in high places. He was perhaps the most successful attorney of his time, both in the number of favorable verdicts won for his clients and in his financial return. But Ingersoll remained skeptical of the practice of law throughout that long, profitable, and successful practice. To him, it was not an instrument for seeing that justice was done; all too often, it was instrument for the perpetuation of injustice, a means of enslaving the weak for the benefit of the strong, and a performance based upon sham, dishonesty, deceit, and trickery. His first recorded observation on the workings of the law, in a letter to his brother John, written while he was teaching in Tennessee, indicates the contempt he felt even before he became a lawyer:

. . . It is rather lonesome here all alone and in a slave state at that where the very air seems to be chained. Nothing but nigers [*sic*] nigers all the time. I have attended one negro sale where a woman and two little children were sold and parted. (She was the mother of both the children) and one was about two and the other three years old, and yet the Law of the state on that subject is "That no child shall be sold or separated from its mother till it shall have attained the age of eight years." But the Law is of no force for who will prosecute the breakers of the Law. It is an indictable offense and might only be taken notice of by a Grand Jury, and it is for the interest of Grand Jurors (Being all slave holders) to say nothing about it so as to sell themselves and let others sell children from mothers. Well that's enough Law for one letter.[1]

After having established himself in the profession in Peoria, his cynicism continued as he wrote to his brother John, who was by then a practicing physician, "We have a very nice office and lighted with gas. Gas you know is an excellent thing in law, in fact indispensable." A few months later he described his practice to John and, at the same time, revealed one of the major attractions which he found in the profession:

... Last week and week before criminal court was in session. Clark and I had most of the business. I defended three men for robbery and had the good luck to clear them all. Everybody thought surely that they would take a little trip to Alton and seemed surprised that I cleared them. There is not a single lawyer in town that is a good speaker, and Clark and I have already the reputation of being the only criminal lawyers at the bar. I think we are going to make lots of money. Since I have been here we have taken in in cash about one hundred dollars per month and charged on good men about one hundred and fifty or two hundred more. We are defending a man here who has been indicted for perjury. He is well off and can afford to pay us. He has made us a deed to six city lots worth at least two hundred and fifty dollars apiece. So you see that is a tolerable large fee. I think we shall have no difficulty in clearing him, though it is rather a hard case. . . .[2]

Seven years later, after having returned from the Civil War, he asserted that "The thing called law I am daily losing respect for . . ."; and, although he averaged between twenty-five and fifty thousand dollars a year from his practice, his contempt continued to the point where, as late as 1892, when his New York practice was particularly profitable, he insisted that he had to make enough money so that he could get out of the business of law, an occupation that consisted of quibbling, listening to liars, reading idiotic decisions, and listening to judges "as ignorant as Balaam's jackass."

Ingersoll's attitude toward the law, together with his continual success in its practice, illustrates one of the basic paradoxes in his nature. Although Ingersoll's apologists have asserted that he never accepted a criminal case in which he was not confident that the defendant was innocent, the facts indicate that his attitude was pragmatic rather than idealistic. He subscribed to the belief that any man was entitled to the best defense that he could afford; and he was willing to provide it. He rarely commented out of the court about either the guilt or the innocence of his client; almost invariably, his comments were that he had or had not secured an acquittal; and many of his critics insisted that his only interest was money, particularly in the notorious *Star Route* trials, one of the longest, most complicated, most politically dominated trials in the history of American jurisprudence. Ingersoll's fees were indeed high, whether in criminal cases or in corporation and will cases, which were less spectacular but more profitable; but his clients invariably received the high measure of legal and psychological insight and histrionic ability that Ingersoll used without reservation in each case.

The combination of high fees and successful cases indicates that the apparent paradox is actually not paradoxical at all, that in attempting to define the significance of Ingersoll's law career both critics and apologists have generated more smoke than light in their heated debates. Actually, in spite of his distaste for the profession—a dislike engendered by his natural intellectual honesty and fastidiousness—Ingersoll was quite consistent in his career from the beginning. Like many other poor but bright and ambitious boys of his time and place, including Abraham Lincoln, he was attracted to the law not because it offered the opportunity to make a reality out of an elusive, abstract justice but because it offered respectability, an adequate livelihood, and, in both cases, an opportunity to enter politics. Having accepted the law on those terms, he continued on the same terms to the end by selling his abilities as he would any other commodity. His frequent references to his practice as a business rather than as a profession were obviously not accidental, as his awareness of the nuances of words makes clear.

Ingersoll's abilities as a lawyer were based upon his passion for factual, rational analysis before generalizing; his gift of almost total recall at any given moment; and his effectiveness as a speaker. Rather than seeking support for his cause in the dusty volumes of precedent, he sought it in careful preparation, even in such highly technical fields as anatomy and surgery; in his phenomenal ability to remember and use the slightest detail; and, above all, in his oratorical skill, with which he presented the facts as he saw and interpreted them, demolished his opponents, and led the jury to accept his conclusion.

In each of his major cases, his opening and closing addresses to the jury were examples of Ingersoll at his best; and each of them illustrates his concepts of justice versus legality, the rights of the individual, and the often elusive distinction between guilt and innocence. Just as he was suspicious and resentful of the aura of mystery and sanctity with which ministers and theologians surrounded their institutions and theological structures, he was equally suspicious of the same tendency among lawyers and jurists. Equally intolerant of their pretensions to sanctity as well as the trappings of robes and high benches, he equated those pretensions with the ritualistic and sacramental devices and trappings of the church.

At the same time, he was well aware that his reputation as an agnostic was a singularly difficult handicap. Not only did it frequently prejudice judges and juries against him, but his opponents often did not hesitate to use his unorthodoxy as a weapon with which to enlarge or prey upon prejudices that may have been dormant. At times, he commented, he felt that he rather than his client was on trial and that the client's fate would be decided by the attitude of judge and jury toward his own agnosticism.

Nevertheless, in spite of his often expressed contempt for the legal profession and his awareness of the shortcomings of an institution surrounded by superstition and operated by human beings, he had a great deal of faith in the potential for justice inherent in the law. In 1891, he wrote to a young man seeking advice that he thought the law a good profession—although again he emphasized the business aspects of the practice—and, in his brief essay "The Law's Delay," he made clear not only his insight into the shortcomings of the institution but also the ideal which the law must uphold if it is to have meaning. A blend of idealism and practicality, humanitarian libertarianism and dispassionate logicality, the essay makes no contribution to the scholarship of the law, but it emphasizes what Ingersoll believed it must be:

The object of a trial is not to convict—neither is it to acquit. The object is to ascertain the truth by legal testimony and in accordance with law. . . .

. . . We must remember that revenge is always in haste, and that justice can always afford to wait until the evidence is actually heard. . . .

There should be no delay except that which is caused by taking the time to find the truth. Without such delay, courts become mobs, before which, trials in a legal sense are impossible.

. . . The appeal, where the accused is guilty, does not take the sword from the State, but it is a shield for the innocent.

The State in which a criminal cannot have an impartial trial is not civilized. People who demand the conviction of the accused without regard to the forms of law are savages.

The State should never seek revenge; neither should it put in peril the life or liberty of the accused for the sake of a hasty trial, or by the denial of appeal. (XI, 501–3)

Perhaps most significant is his attitude toward the convicted criminal, an attitude based not upon legality but upon morality and concern for the criminal as well as for society. He believed that criminals should be reformed rather than punished and that the prisons themselves should be reformed to make reformation possible rather than the impossibility he saw it to be. Like Dorothea Dix and others of her reformist conviction, he regarded the criminal as a human being who had committed a crime and who, unless dangerous or depraved, was not beyond reformation.

His major cases included the *Munn* trial of 1876, the *Star Route* trials of 1882–83, the *Davis* will case which began in 1891 and was not concluded until after his death, and the *Russell* will case, just two months before his death. In each case, his major arguments rather than the skill and wit of his examination, cross-examination, debate, and manipulation carry the weight of his cause, although he certainly did not neglect either the routine or the momentary dramas of the courtroom. Often, however, the routine was left to his legal associates, and the arguments, like his appearances on the lecture platform, were carefully staged with disarming simplicity so that the dramatic impact of his presence, as well as that of his oratorical skill, might combine persuasively with the wide range of his argument.

I   *The* Munn *Case*

The *Munn* case was especially demanding of his combined abilities because it involved a sordid plot to defraud the government of the revenue tax on whiskey. Daniel W. Munn, deputy supervisor of Internal Revenue, was accused of defrauding the government of millions of dollars; and he hired Ingersoll to defend him. In an age increasingly prohibitionist, with the Temperance organizations increasingly powerful and vocal, Ingersoll knew that he was dealing with a case fraught with the hidden danger of that prohibitionist sentiment. Therefore, in his closing remarks he determined to attack that prejudice head-on and to defuse its potential explosiveness before turning to logical and emotional appeals:

. . . The evidence has been gone over by my associates, and arguments have been submitted to you which, in my judgement, are perfectly convincing as far as the innocence of this defendant is concerned. I am aware, however, that there is a prejudice against a case of this character. I am aware that there is a prejudice against any man engaged in the manufacture of alcohol. I know there is a prejudice against a case of this kind; and there is a very good reason for it. I believe to a certain degree with the district attorney in this case, who has said that every man who makes whiskey is demoralized. I believe, gentlemen, to a certain degree, it demoralizes those who make it, those who sell it, and those who drink it. I believe from the time it issues from the coiled and poisonous worm of the distillery, until it empties into the hell of crime, dishonor, and death, that it demoralizes everybody that touches it. I do not believe anybody can comtemplate the subject without becoming prejudiced against this liquid crime. . . . (X, 7–8)

After skillfully identifying himself with the popular and respectable prejudice and, incidentally, providing the prohibitionists with evidence of support which he did not feel, Ingersoll turned to attacking the testimony of the government's chief witness, an alleged co-conspirator who had turned state's evidence. After examining the testimony in critical and logical detail, he attacked it:

Perjury poisons the wells of truth, the sources of justice. Perjury leaps from the hedges of circumstance, from the walls of fact, to assassinate justice and innocence. Perjury is the basest and meanest and most cowardly of crimes. What can it do? Perjury can change the common air that we breathe into the axe of an executioner. Perjury out of this air can forge manacles for free hands. Perjury out of a single word can make a hangman's rope and noose. Perjury out of a word can build a scaffold upon which the great and noble must suffer. . . .

Is there any safety in the world if you take the testimony of these men, expecially when character avails nothing? Is there any safety in human society if you will take the testimony of a perjured man? Is there any safety in living among mankind if this is the law,—if the statement of a confessed conspirator makes the character of a great and good man worthless? . . . (X, 20)

After continuing the attack on the nature and validity of the testimony and reliability of the witness, examining the record in detail as he did so, he turned to his final weapon: sheer emotional sentimentality and sympathy:

I want you to try this case according to the evidence and nothing else. I want you to say whether you believe the testimony of these conspirators and scoundrels. . . . [I] f you bring in a verdict of guilty I want you to be able to defend yourselves when you go to the defendant and tell him: "We found you guilty upon a man's testimony who admitted that he was a thief; who admitted that he was a perjurer; who admitted that he hired others to swear lies, and who committed crimes without number year after year." I want you to say whether that is an excuse to give to him. Is it an excuse to give to his pallid, invalid wife? Is it an excuse to give to his father, eighty years old, trembling upon the verge of the grave: "I sent your son to the penitentiary upon the evidence of a convicted thief?" I say is it an excuse to give to his weeping wife? Is it an excuse to give to his child: "I sent your father to the penitentiary upon the evidence of Jacob Rehm"? There is not one of you can go to the child, or to the sick wife, or to the old man, or to the defendant himself, and without the blush of shame say: "I sent you to the penitentiary upon the evidence of Jacob Rehm." You cannot do it. It is not in human nature to do it. (X, 31—33)

Although his indictment of the prosecution's chief witness remained his chief weapon throughout the argument, nevertheless Ingersoll did not hesitate to use any weapon at his command, including an air of seeming simplicity and naïveté as he concluded his speech with references to reiterations and amplifications of arguments that he asserted he had forgotten. Obviously, however, he had not; instead, in the final minutes he once more repeated his major arguments: the dangers of prejudice; the admittedly and allegedly dishonest character of the chief prosecution witness; and the introduction of a new element—patriotism:

I care everything for my client. I care everything for his honor, and more than that, gentlemen, I love the United States of America. I love this Government, I love this form of government and I do not want to see the sources of government poisoned. I do not want to see a state of things in the United States of America whereby a man can be consigned to a dungeon upon the testimony of a robber and thief, simply upon a political issue, simply by the testimony of some man who wishes to purchase immunity at the price of another's liberty and honor. (X, 34)

The effectiveness of Ingersoll's handling of the case in general and of his closing speech in particular was demonstrated with the verdict of acquittal. The speech itself has found a permanent place in the *Collected Works,* where it demonstrates the pattern into which Ingersoll's speeches fell: the combination of logic, emotion, presence, and carefully staged simplicity that he found equally effective on the lecture platform. The legal aspects of both Ingersoll's handling of the case and of his re-examination of the testimony in the final address rarely indicate more than routine competence; however, his demonstrated psychological insight into the particular demands of the situation and his ability to capture the sympathy of the jury as effectively as he did in this case are the talents of a master showman.

Although his denunciation of alcohol returned to haunt him as proof of his sympathy for prohibition and to force him to reiterate that prohibition was a denial of man's freedom and reason, Ingersoll was proud of the *Munn* case and was pleased with its results: it gave him a national reputation as a criminal lawyer. Combined with the national political reputation which he had acquired in the election campaign of 1876, the case enable him to move to the much greater and much more lucratice practice in Washington, D. C., where he once more joined his brother Ebon Clark, who had remained there after serving in Congress.

II   *The* Star Route *Cases*

As in the *Munn* case, Ingersoll's major successes in the larger national arena were primarily personal rather than legal victories. In this category was his participation in the *Star Route* cases, which were also based upon accusations of defrauding the government. If the *Munn* case was potentially dangerous, the *Star Route* cases were potentially explosive because any scandal would inevitably involve Ingersoll's own Republican party. Although Ingersoll's ensuing efforts did much to bring about the break in his relations with James G. Blaine, whom he had supported so strongly in 1876, he nevertheless threaded his way through the most scandalous trial in American history to that time; and both he and the party emerged safely, although with some damage to the reputation of both.

The Star Routes were rural mail routes in the South and West that were operated by private contractors. The Post Office Department, under authorization from Congress, was empowered to adjust the compensation to contractors who improved services or otherwise showed need. Serving under President Grant, Thomas J. Brady, second assistant postmaster general, began awarding contracts on a political basis, many of which were then subcontracted and the profit retained. Upon ninety-three of them Brady authorized increases totaling two million dollars, to the profit of a number of Republican regulars. Although, when the scandal broke and the trials began, President Garfield insisted upon full investigation and prosecution, leading members of Congress and members of his Cabinet supported the accused: evidence disappeared, officeholders refused to aid the prosecution, and prosecution plans were secretly betrayed to the accused. Evidence of a scandal reaching into every area of the party, including the financing of the election of 1880, was so overwhelming that it led Ellis P. Oberhaltzer to comment that for Ingersoll to believe in the innocence of his clients should have been more difficult than for him to accept the revelations of Moses and the prophets.

The first trial, from May to September, 1882, on the specific charge of conspiring to defraud the government, resulted in conviction for two, acquittal for two, and in a hung jury for four. The patent ridiculousness of the results led to the second trial, lasting from December, 1882, to June, 1883. In both of them, Ingersoll found maximum opportunity to utilize his talents. The complexity of the case alone, involving millions of dollars, the conflicting testimony of highly placed men, the technicalities of complex statutes, and the handicap of a party actually prosecuting itself made the role of prosecutor and defense counsel decisive. Among the talented array for the defense in both cases, Ingersoll was without question the star.

In his closing argument Ingersoll used the basic pattern that had served in the *Munn* case. But he made even stronger his disassociation from the potentially prejudicial issue, in this case the magnitude of the fraud and, more important, the fact that it was perpetrated against the government of the United States, than he had his disassociation from the taint of alcohol:

Let us understand each other at the very threshold. For one I am as much opposed to official dishonesty as any man in this world. The taxes in this country are paid by labor and by industry, and they should be collected and disbursed by integrity. The man that is untrue to his official oath, the man that is untrue to the position the people have honored him with, ought to be punished. I have not one word to say in defence of any man who I believe has robbed the Treasury of the United States. I want it understood in the first place that we are not defending; that we are not excusing; that we are not endeavoring to palliate in the slightest degree dishonesty in any Government official. (X, 39)

This disassociation of himself from the possibility of his clients' guilt was far stronger, far blunter than the high-flown rhetoric of his denunciation of alcohol; but Ingersoll went further: he made the case a test of his own personal integrity as well when he insisted that "I will not defend any citizen who has committed what I believe to be a fraud upon the Treasury of this Government" (X, 39).

After having made his personal as well as his legal commitment clear, Ingersoll turned to the defense of the era, an age that had become increasingly associated in the popular mind not only with the political corruption of the Grant adminstration and now the Star Route scandals, but with a national demoralization that, stemming from the Civil War, had contaminated the life of the country itself. To Ingersoll, that view was arrant nonsense; and he moved to the attack, citing the record of the nation in freeing a people at tremendous self-sacrifice. At the same time, he subtly reminded the jury that the Republican party was responsible for the new birth of freedom under law as he appealed to sheer patriotic pride:

> When we broke the shackles from four millions of men, women and children it did not demoralize us. When we changed the hut of the slave into the castle of the freeman it did not demoralize us. When we put the protecting arm of the law about that hut and the flag of this nation above it, it was not very demoralizing. . . . That war was the noblest affirmation of humanity in the history of this world. We are a greater people, we are a grander people, than we were before that war. The war repealed statutes that had been made by robbery and theft. It made this country the home of MAN. We were not demoralized. (X, 40)

If the temper of the times, as defined by critics as varied as clergymen and politicians, writers and countrymen, was only remotely related to the guilt or innocence of his clients, Ingersoll found it the opportunity for one of his most persuasive appeals. But more than that, he used the opportunity to lead directly into the charges of corruption leveled against the times and to deny them through the same prideful patriotic affirmation:

> This country is not distinguished for corruption. No true patriot believes it. This country is distinguished for something else. . . . I always supposed that we were distinguished for free schools, for free speech, for just laws; not for corruption. A country covered with schoolhouses, where the children of the poor are put upon an exact equality with those of the rich, is not distinguished for corruption. And yet in the name of this universal corruption you are appealed to to become also corrupt. . . . (X, 41)

With the suggestion, supported by his personal integrity and by his faith in the nation and in its servants, his clients, that corruption might creep into the findings if the jury were not wary, Ingersoll then lectured the jurymen upon the law, upon their duties, and upon the planted suggestion that there could be but one honest verdict—a verdict that might be publicly unpopular. He turned, too, to the duties of the lawyer, insisting that it was to make the case clear to the jury, a statement that had no overtone of irony in spite of the fact that he then began to marshal facts, conjecture, statutes, precedents, denials, and allegations of deceit in such an array that no jury composed of laymen, regardless of intelligence, could hope to follow them clearly. At times, however, he summed up with disarming simplicity: "Suspicion, gentlemen, is not evidence. You want to go at it with this idea. Whatever a man does, the presumption is it is an honest act until the contrary is shown. These men wrote letters. They had a right to do it. They met. They had a right to meet. They entered into contracts. They had a right to do it, no matter whether they were dated or not dated. . . . (X, 97).

As Ingersoll closed his examination of the evidence, he concluded that his clients had been proved guilty of only one thing: of carrying the mails efficiently and courageously—conveniently ignoring the fact that his clients had themselves been quite remote from that activity: "You ought to be there sometimes in the winter when the wind comes down with an unbroken sweep of three or four thousand miles, and then tell me what you think it is worth to carry the mails?" (X, 129).

I believe in carrying the mails. I believe in the diffusion of intelligence. . . . We are a nation that believes in intelligence.

We believe in daily mail. That is about the only blessing we get from the General Government, excepting the privilege of paying taxes. Free mail, substantially free, is a blessing. (X, 140)

There remained one major appeal for Ingersoll to make, and a prosecution remark about the presence of one defendant's wife sitting beside him provided the opportunity:

. . . this prosecution, this Government, these attorneys representing the majesty of the Republic, representing the only real Republic that ever existed, have asked you, gentlemen of the jury, not only to violate the law of the land, they have asked you to violate the law of nature. They have maligned mercy. They have laughed at mercy. They have trampled upon the holiest human ties, and they have even made light of the fact that a wife in this trial has sat by her husband's side. Think of it. (X, 140)

The best of Ingersoll's magnificent irrelevancy was to come as he led the jury into what should be thought about it:

There is a painting in the Louvre, a painting of desolation; of despair and love. It represents the night of the crucifixion. The world is represented in shadow. The stars are dead, and yet in the darkness is seen a kneeling form. It is Mary Magdalene with loving lips and hands pressed against the bleeding feet of Christ. The skies were never dark enough nor starless enough; the storm was never fierce enough nor wild enough, the quick bolts of heaven were never lurid enough, and arrows of slander never flew thick enough to drive a noble woman from her husband's side. And so it is in all of human speech, the *holiest word* is WIFE. (X,140)

Regardless of theological implications, which may or may not have been deliberately included in this concluding part of the speech, other implications were clear, as the prosecutor was quick to observe. A comparison with Mary Magdalene opened areas of speculation that could be other than flattering to any wife so compared; but, perhaps more important, the reference and implied comparison to the Crucifixion was ethically dubious in the light of Ingersoll's well-known convictions about the reality and significance of the event.

Whatever the intent or the ethics of the statement, the results were what Ingersoll intended. Impartial as well as biased observers reported a strong emotional impact on the courtroom as many of those, including ladies attracted to the trial out of curiosity or out of a desire to hear Ingersoll, were seen crying as the courtroom burst into spontaneous applause. It was without question one of Ingersoll's most successful courtroom appearances in spite of the ambiguity of the mixed and illogical sentence. Nevertheless, the fact that only two of eight defendants were convicted was a tribute to Ingersoll's effectiveness and—in the view of some observers—an indictment of the jury's intelligence.

The second *Star Route* trial provides the opportunity to contrast Ingersoll's approach and techniques in his opening and closing remarks with the closing remarks in the earlier. Normally, Ingersoll did not make opening addresses in major cases; he preferred that others do it, but in this case he did so. When the second trial opened, the atmosphere was no less threatening than it had been earlier; and Ingersoll's reputation had suffered from his association with the case, primarily among liberals and humanists who had staunchly defended him in the past. Nevertheless, because of a shift in emphasis in both opening and closing addresses as well as a change in the popular attitude toward the scandals, Ingersoll emerged with his reputation restored and with all his clients acquitted.

His opening address followed the same general organizational pattern that he had followed before, with one major difference in structure and another in form. In both the opening and closing sections of the speech, he devoted himself to restrained, largely unemotional lectures to the jury on the nature of the jury system and on the duties of each individual juror. Between them was a statement of the case, the indictment, and the evidence as the defense saw them to be. He reiterated that the only guilt that could be proven was the guilt of having carried the mails faithfully and democratically to rich and poor alike. But in his indictment of the indictment, Ingersoll introduced a new charge against the government: the expense of the case, which was being increasingly criticized by the press and citizens at large:

. . . I say to you today that the entire profit has been *less than* ten thousand dollars, not enough to pay ten witnesses of the government. Our profits have not been one-fiftieth of the expense of the government in this prosecution—not one-fiftieth, and I say this, gentlemen, knowing what I am saying. It is charged by the Government that these gentlemen were conspirators; that they dragged the robes of office in the mire of rascality; that they swore lies; that they made false petitions; that they forged the names of citizens; that they did all this for the paltry profit of ten thousand dollars. . . (X, 181)

Ingersoll's insistence was then to be that the government was persecuting rather than prosecuting, and he then pointed out the source of such misguided expensive zeal that in itself was criminal in its results. The persecution stemmed from attempts at reform, which, Ingersoll implied, was often an attempt to distract the public attention from activities even more questionable:

. . . And the moment this reform administration swept into power they cut down the service on these routes. They not only did that, but they refused to pay the month's extra pay, and they committed all this villainy in the name of reform. And do you know that some of the meanest things in this world have been done in the name of reform? They used to say that patriotism was the last refuge of a scoundrel. I think reform is. And whenever I hear a small politican talking about reform, borrowing soap to wash his official hands, with his mouth full and his memory glutted with the rascality of somebody else I begin to suspect him; I begin to think that that gentleman is preparing to steal something. So much, then, for the conspiracy. . . . (X, 181)

In his final paragraph he refrained from sentimentality but not emotionalism as he tried to bring each of the jurors personally into the case:

... It is for you to say, gentlemen, whether a man should be found guilty on inference; whether a man shall be deprived of his liberty by prejudice. It is for you to say whether reputation shall be destroyed by malice and by ignorance. It is for you to say whether a man who fought to sustain this Government shall not have the protection of the laws. It is for you [indicating a juror] and it is for you [indicating another juror] and you [indicating another juror] and you [indicating another juror] to say whether a man who fought to take the chains off your body shall have chains put upon his by your prejudice and by your ignorance. It is for you to say whether you will be guided by law, by evidence, by justice, by reason, or whether you will be controlled by fear, by prejudice, by reason, or whether you will be controlled by fear, by prejudice, and by official power. (X, 214–15)

The restraint evident in Ingersoll's opening address was also evident throughout the trial in strong contrast to the heavily emotional and sentimental atmosphere earlier. The trial covered almost six months; much popular sentiment had begun to support the underdog defendants; and the talk of corruption and the eagerness for reform had begun to be dissipated. Ingersoll was obviously determined to win upon the evidence rather than with the help of popular emotionalism that might once more turn and condemn his clients. Much of his time was devoted, therefore, to examining the testimony and evidence in detail and then to lecturing the jury upon the laws of evidence in relationship to specific details. Only occasionally did Ingersoll's righteous wit shine, as in his abrupt, condescending dismissal of the testimony of a key witness:

... I shall not take up your time in the remainder of my speech by commenting upon Mr. Rerdell. Let us finish his testimony now; let us put him put of sight; let us put him in his coffin, close the lid, nail it down:

First nail—affidavit of June 20, 1881; drive it in.

Second nail—the letter of July 5, 1882, when he says that affidavit of 1881 was made by the persuasion of Bosler; drive it in.

Third nail—affidavit of July 13, 1882, where he swears that they were all perfectly innocent.

Fourth nail—the pencil memorandum; drive that in.

Fifth nail—the tabular statement that gave thirty-three and one-third per cent to Brady; drive it in.

Sixth nail—his pretended letter to Bosler telling about the advice of Brady; drive that in.

Seventh nail—the letter he pretends that Dorsey, on the 13th of May, 1879, wrote to Bosler, the copies being made by Miss White; drive that in.

Wind his corpse up in the balance sheets from the red books made by Donnelly.

Then you want a plate for his coffin. Let us paste right on there the Chico letter, April 3, 1878.

Now we want grave-stones. Let us take the red books, put one at his head and one at his feet.

And let his epitaph, written upon the red book placed at his head, be—

Up to this moment I have been faithful to every trust.

My prayer to Gabriel is, "When you pass over that grave don't blow." Let him sleep. There are, there never were, there never will be twelve honest men who will deprive any citizen of his liberty upon the evidence of a man like Mr. Rerdell. It never happened; it never will. (X, 371–72)

Such devastating dismissal of testimony and of the man who gave it was dispassionate but powerful in its insistence of fraud and trickery too ignoble to consider except with contempt. In other instances, he used the same technique with the same effectiveness. But the bulk of the address was devoted to a close examination, point by point, of the transcript of prosecution testimony and the painstaking refutation of each point. A very carefully prepared address, it was particularly difficult because the record of the trial already ran to thousands of pages.

Unquestionably one of Ingersoll's most exhaustive cases, it depended for its success as much upon the careful examination of each point, the plausible explanation of each, and the apparently open honesty of the defense—with which Ingersoll identified himself thoroughly in his terminology—as it did on the effectiveness of presentation. Only in his final paragraphs did he turn to the sentimental, and then it was restrained in comparison to what had gone before:

. . . It is for you to say whether there shall be left to these defendants and to those they love, a future of agony, of grief and tears.

Nothing beneath the stars of heaven is so profoundly sad as the wreck of a human being. Nothing is so profoundly mournful as a home that has been covered with shame—a wife that is worse than widowed—children worse than orphaned. Nothing in this world is so infinitely sad as a verdict that will cast a stain upon children yet unborn. . . .

I want a verdict in accordance with the evidence. I want a verdict in accordance with the law. I want a verdict that will relieve my clients from the agony of two years. I want a verdict that will drive the darkness from the heart of the wife. I want a verdict that will take the cloud of agony from the roof and the home. I want a verdict that will fill the coming days and nights with joy. I want a verdict that, like a splendid flower, will fill the future of their lives with a sense of thankfulness and gratitude to you, gentlemen, one and all. (X, 528—29)

The conclusion of the trial was considered a personal triumph for Ingersoll. In spite of continued rumors and assertions of guilt on the part of the defendants, often expanded to suggest astronomical sums which Ingersoll had presumably received as fees and expenses, the press and popular opinion generally conceded that Ingersoll had provided a masterful defense. The stigma that had been attached to him after the first trial disappeared, and his personal identification with the case, crucial in the courtroom, was nonexistent outside it. The personal nature of Ingersoll's victory was reported by the New York *Sun:*

. . . When Colonel Ingersoll came out of the Court House a crowd gathered in front of him, and then one stout-lunged, broad shouldered man cried out. "Three cheers for Colonel Ingersoll." There was a wild scene of tiger-like cheering from the excited crowd. This demonstration was a personal compliment to the Colonel, for when the defendants passed out there was not the slightest sound of approval or disapproval beyond the congratulations of personal friends. Colonel Ingersoll stood on the broad steps of the Court House and smiled with the benevolent air of a popular orator in front of a congenial crowd, and laughed outright when some over-enthusiastic admirer called "Speech, speech." [3]

Although the country at large, including major newspapers, were convinced that justice had not been done, Ingersoll's reputation as a skilled defense attorney was greatly enhanced; and the success was largely responsible for his moving to New York in 1885 and for his accepting less demanding, less sensational, but more profitable work in corporation and will cases. Ingersoll, who was almost immediately aware of its effects on his future, wrote that "The verdict is considered as a great victory for me. I never took such an interest in a case. I felt that it was life or death with me. . . . I defied them from the first and wiped the floor up with them at last. . . ." [4] Rumored doubts about his role in the trials never appeared in his writings, and for more than a decade he expressed his pride in his part in the trial. It was a case that he had to win in order to vindicate himself, and he did so with glory.

In less spectacular cases, he was no less successful; but his continued successes enhanced his fame and his practice, enabling him to participate, if only indirectly, in the great railroad, industrial, and telegraph wars that characterized his era. The most celebrated of these was the suit in 1887 of the Merchants' and Bankers' Telegraph Company against Jay Gould's Western Union. In its drive for monopoly, Western Union had seized its rival's property and destroyed its wires. In the ensuing suit, Ingersoll accused Western Union of consisting of millionaire-led mobs stifling competition by ignoring the right of the public to communicate. The successful verdict gave Ingersoll's clients a judgement of $1,500,000—and Ingersoll a tidy fee.

III *The* Reynolds *Case*

Only once, in 1885, did Ingersoll defend a client on trial for the same beliefs that Ingersoll professed. In the *Reynolds* blasphemy case in Morristown, New Jersey, Charles B. Reynolds, a Freethought lecturer, had been indicted for blasphemy; and Ingersoll, who served without fee, based his defense on the premise that to speak out honestly and in accordance with one's beliefs was no crime. Although he used the opportunity to attack the orthodox doctrines which were noxious to him as well as to his client, his major plea was for liberty of conscience and speech. The antiblasphemy statute was unconstitutional, he insisted, and he violated it himself in the courtroom.

Although his plea was an eloquent argument in defense of freedom, Reynolds was found guilty and fined twenty-five dollars and costs, which Ingersoll paid with a flourish. In his closing argument, he gave his famous definition of blasphemy, an indictment of superstition and injustice, concluding with patriotic fervor that

I sincerely hope that it will never be necessary again, under the flag of the United States—that flag for which has been shed the bravest and best blood of the world—under that flag maintained by Washington, by Jefferson, by Franklin and by Lincoln—under that flag in defence of which New Jersey poured out her best and bravest blood—I hope it will never be necessary again for a man to stand before a jury and plead for the Liberty of Speech. (XI, 117)

There is no question in this case of any possible doubts in Ingersoll's mind: he was on the side of justice, honesty, and freedom. However, the statute remained; and in lecture tours in the state Ingersoll took delight in flaunting it by proclaiming his uncertainty about his beliefs and then pointing to the statute as the source of the uncertainty.

IV *The* Davis *Will Case*

Among his major will cases was the celebrated *Davis* case in Butte, Montana, in 1891, in which Ingersoll's clients contested the validity of a will disposing of six to eight million dollars. Again, Ingersoll seemed on trial for his beliefs as well as for his forensic skill since both the judge and the opposing attorney made them issues in the case. Although ultimately a divided jury led to a compromise settlement out of court, Ingersoll's fee was not paid until after his death, when Mrs. Ingersoll was forced to file suit. Particularly interesting in the Butte case is the account of Ingersoll as he was seen by the local paper:

The matchless eloquence of Ingersoll! Where will one look for the like of it? What other man living has the faculty of blending wit and humor, pathos and fact and logic with such exquisite grace, or with such impressive force? . . . To a modern audience, at least Demosthenes on the Crown would seem a pretty poor sort of an affair by the side of Ingersoll on the Davis will. It was a great effort, and its chief greatness lay in its extreme simplicity.

Ingersoll stepped up to the jurors as near as he could get and kept slowly walking up and down before them. At times he would single out a single juryman, stop in front of him, gaze steadily into his face and direct his remarks for a minute or two to that one man alone. . . . If the jury could have retired immediately upon the conclusion of Ingersoll's argument, there is little doubt as to what the verdict would have been.

. . . In doing this he adopted a conversational tone and kept pressing the point until the juror he was working upon nodded his head in approval.

The crowd . . . enjoyed Ingersoll's speech immensely, and only respect for the proprieties . . . prevented frequent bursts of applause as an accompaniment to the frequent bursts of eloquence.[5]

In these major cases and in all of Ingersoll's minor cases it becomes evident throughout the record of each that Ingersoll was neither a scholar of the law nor a legal philosopher. He was a competent attorney who was well versed in the laws of evidence and who was diligent in the examination of the record. He did his homework conscientiously, whether personally or through the medium of his assistants; and he had the ability to master and remember complicated briefs quite easily. At the same time, he had, as has been noted, no great reverence for the law itself and a great deal of contempt for its human as well as structural weaknesses. Although his apologists insist that he was primarily interested in impartial justice and that he had no real interest in victory, there is little evidence in the record to substantiate those assertions. Indeed, there is more evidence to suggest the opposite: that Ingersoll was interested in victory; that he saw the legal profession as a business rather than a crusade for justice; and that he used whatever techniques were necessary, including sheer sentimental nonsense and semantic trickery, to win his cases. No matter what the case, Ingersoll was not interested in other than victory, particularly, as in the *Star Route* trials, when he had identified himself personally with the outcome.

In spite of all of these qualities, most of which he shared with countless other lawyers, Ingersoll was a great trial lawyer. In his case, the difference between mediocrity and greatness lay in his theatrical sense of drama and of timing; in his instinct for eloquent simplicity; and, above all, in his talents as an orator. Each plea was for him much more than a mere plea; it was a performance. His goal was not merely to persuade logically but to lead the jurors—and the audience—to identify empathetically with his client. Even in the most hostile courtroom Ingersoll was able to use the atmosphere of hostility to his own advantage. Seeming simplicity, sharp wit, an air of confidence and intimacy, a strong dramatic instinct, and an eloquent mastery of voice, language, syntax, and phraseology, combined with a forceful presence, made him perhaps the greatest trial lawyer of his day. With his obvious talents, there is no need to insist, as do many of his apologists, that he was either a crusader or a philosopher—or to make him other than he was.

CHAPTER 3

"Ideas are greater than parties . . ."

T HE failure of Ingersoll's modest bid for the governorship of Illinois in 1868 neither decreased his interest in politics nor weakened his allegiance to the Republican party. It did mean, however, that personal political ambitions were put behind him. To insist, however, that his continued role in the political life of the party and of the nation was the result of either his intellectual integrity and deep patriotism, as his apologists insist, or his self-seeking drive for power, as his critics maintain, is nonsense; as in his attitude toward his profession, there is no possible simplistic interpretation of his ambiguous, often paradoxical attitude, toward his party, its candidates, and his country.

It is equally evident that Ingersoll was not a political philosopher. The depth of his devotion to what he saw as the American ideal is unquestioned, and in theory and practice he devoted much attention to making that ideal a reality; but his attempts, his successes, and his failures were largely based upon acceptance of the interpretations of those ideals made by others rather than upon his own innovations in either theory or practice. As in his role in the legal institution of the country, his major political contributions were his talents as an orator rather than as a theorist. At the same time, it is evident that his own personal political preferences, prejudices, and feuds sometimes played a major role in the extent to which he supported or failed to support party nominees.

In 1868, for example, after his defeat for the gubernatorial nomination, he refused to speak for General Palmer's candidacy for the governorship, nor did he give vocal support to other nominees for state offices. He did, however, support Ulysses S. Grant for the presidency; and, at the same time, he worked diligently for the re-election to Congress of his brother, Ebon Clark. In 1870, he again supported Ebon strongly; and, upon his defeat, Ebon returned to private law practice in the partnership until he died in 1879.

During the years prior to 1876, Ingersoll's political activities and reputation had not become nationally prominent, and his speeches were restricted largely to the Midwest. He did, however, enjoy a regional reputation; and he was particularly adept at a technique which became known as "waving the bloody shirt," an attempt to channel the residual animosities of the Civil War into partisan political support. For Ingersoll, largely as a result of his courtroom experience, the technique was logical as well as effective as he indicted the Democrats as the party of slavery, of treason, and of permanent enmity toward human liberty. So completely did he make the identification at times that the political arena became an apparent extension of the military campaigns; the Democrats consisted of Lee's veterans and the Republicans of those who had marched on Richmond and to the sea.

Nevertheless, there were occasions upon which Ingersoll rose above party—or, perhaps more accurately, above partisanship—in his awareness that practicality sometimes takes precedent over principle. In addressing a meeting of Negroes in Galesburg, Illinois, in 1867, in his capacity as attorney general of the state, he came close to ignoring party politics in a brief speech that is remarkable for its brevity, its obvious sincerity, and its attempt to clarify and communicate. One of the few occasions on which Ingersoll's simplicity was not an artful device but a tribute to the awe with which he approached the concept of human freedom, it is not condescending, as was so much of the rhetoric addressed to the Negro at the time. Instead, he talked about the concept as it was, as it became a reality through the agency of dedicated men, and as it pointed out the path of the future. He began by examining the reality of slavery in the human experience as it antedated the concept that was ultimately to destroy it:

Fellow citizens—Slavery has in a thousand forms existed in all ages, and among all people. It is as old as theft and robbery.

Every nation has enslaved its own people, and sold its own flesh and blood. Most of the white race are in slavery today. It has often been said that any man who ought to be free, will be. The men who say this should remember that their ancestors were once cringing, frightened slaves.

When they became sufficiently educated to cease enslaving their own people, they then enslaved the first race they could conquer. . . .

Every excuse that the ingenuity of avarice could devise was believed to be a complete justification, and the great argument of slaveholders in all countries has been that slavery is a divine institution, and thus stealing human beings has always been fortified with a "Thus saith the Lord."

Slavery has been upheld by law and religion in every country. The
word Liberty is not in any creed in the world. Slavery is right according
to the law of man, shouted the judge. It is right according to the law of
God, shouted the priest. . . . (IX, 5–6)

The American situation, he then emphasized, was not unique; it was
part of, rather than apart from, human experience until eventually "we
become grand enough to say, 'Slavery shall be eradicated from the soil
of the Republic.' When we reached this sublime moral height we were
successful . . ." (IX, 8).

The course of events that led to this moral triumph was for Ingersoll
evidence of progress, of the belief that men are "nobler, better and
purer than ever." But, although Ingersoll's faith in progress saw that
change in men's hearts as inevitable, he neither sentimentalized nor
oversimplified the change; and he traced the evolutionary and
revolutionary development of the idea from abstraction to reality
through the actions of men from Thomas Clarkson to John Brown—
men "who were for liberty as a principle and not from mere
necessity–" (IX, 11), men to whom the Negro owed gratitude. Among
these, Ingersoll asserted that the greatest was John Brown: "I say no
man can be greater than the man who bravely and heroically sacrifices
his life for the good of others. No man can be greater than the one who
meets death face to face, and yet will not shrink from what he believes
to be his highest duty. If the black people want a patron saint, let them
take the brave old John Brown" (IX, 12–13).

But Ingersoll was not interested in proselytizing his audience; and,
warning them that "You do not . . . owe a great debt of gratitude to
many of white people," he pointed out the role of both parties in
supporting the Fugitive Slave Law that he had denounced so strongly in
1860, and he insisted that the Emancipation Proclamation was a
historical necessity rather than an altruistic gesture. He insisted, too,
that Negro citizenship was the product of a similar necessity and that
the reality of slavery was still close in the human and American
experience: "I hate to think that all this [inhumanity] was done under
the Constitution of the United States, under the flag of my country,
under the wings of the eagle" (IX, 16).

In a note of genuine humility and wonder, he pondered briefly the
significance of his address, the magnitude of the crime against the
Negro race, and the course of the future:

I wonder that you—the black people—have forgotten all this. I
wonder that you ask a white man to address you on this occasion, when

the history of your connection with the white race is written in your blood and tears—is still upon your flesh, put there by the branding-iron and the lash.

I feel like asking your forgiveness for the wrongs that my race has inflicted upon yours. If, in the future, the wheel of fortune should take a turn, and you should in any country have white men in your power, I pray you not to execute the villainy we have taught you. (IX, 16)

But to Ingersoll all this was prologue, and the future he saw characterized by the performance of freedom—a freedom, however, that he warned could only be sustained by education, by mutual help, and by advancing with determination in the cause of freedom for all men.

Although the speech provided a remarkable opportunity for waving the "bloody shirt," Ingersoll did not do so; only twice did he come close to political partisanship. The audience and the occasion made it inevitable that Ingersoll speak honestly, and, as in 1860, when principle rose above partisanship in his congressional campaign, he did not hesitate to do so.

I   *The Campaign of 1868*

In sharp contrast is the result of his movement onto the stump in the presidential year of 1868. Strongly opposed to Andrew Johnson—he once implored his brother to "be a little more radical today than . . . yesterday"—he strongly supported Grant as the only hope for the eradication of treason and for the protection of freedom. In granting that support, he was truly partisan, but he was convinced that his partisanship was based upon principle. Nevertheless, his stump speeches are closely related in structure and emphasis to his appeals to juries in the courtroom. In effect, on the stump Ingersoll felt that he was appealing to the ultimate jury, and he composed and delivered his speeches accordingly.

The speech at Indianapolis in support of Grant's candidacy for the presidency is a part of the "give 'em hell" political oratorical tradition that played an important part in the democratic political arena of the frontier. But at the same time, as Lincoln did in the best of his stump speeches, Ingersoll transcends that bellicose, largely emotional tradition; he attempts, on one hand, to justify Republican policies and controversial achievements by proving that they are in the American democratic tradition; on the other hand, he attacks the Democrats for departing from the tradition. In structure and achievement, the speech approximates Lincoln's Cooper Union address, which supported the Republicans and indicted the Southerners in the same manner and used the same techniques. This approach, too, is part of the tradition of American political oratory, having been used effectively by Daniel Webster in his acceptance of the Compromise of 1850 and in his denial of the right to secession. It was also the technique used most effectively by Harry S Truman as recently as the presidential campaign of 1948.

The specific accusations of the Democrats which Ingersoll chose to refute were two: the very real charge that, under Lincoln, Republicans used the suspension of *habeas corpus* as a political means of imprisoning Democrats; the second, at least partially imaginary, was that the Republicans had freed Negroes, allowed them to vote and fight, and made them legally citizens. In answering both charges, Ingersoll attempted, as Lincoln had at the Cooper Union, to reverse them and use them against the Democrats, and in both cases, he approximated Lincoln's success.

Ingersoll does not deny the charges; instead, in refuting them he uses a combination of logical justification through American historical precedent and the skillful, defiant waving of the "bloody shirt." The parallel between the revolutionary and Civil War periods to Ingersoll is real:

I lay this down as a proposition, that we had a right to do anything to preserve this Government that our fathers had a right to do to found it. If they had a right to put Tories in jail, to suspend the writ of *habeas corpus,* and on some occasions *corpus,* in order to found this Government, we had a right to put rebels and Democrats in jail and to suspend the writ of *habeas corpus* in order to preserve the Government they thus formed. If they had a right to interfere with the freedom of the press in order that liberty might be planted upon the soil, we had a right to do the same thing to prevent the tree from being destroyed. In a word, we have a right to do anything to preserve this Government which they had a right to do to defend it. (IX, 23)

But Ingersoll did not content himself with generalities, and his documentation of historical precedent is detailed, precise, and convincing as he ranged from a detailed examination of the implications of the Committee of Safety, inaugurated by the Continental Congress, through George Washington's denunciation of those who spoke or acted against the government. In his letter to Governor Cooke of Rhode Island, supporting the restrictive measures adopted by that colony, Washington advocated their extension to all other colonies—a measure that Ingersoll insisted was necessary in the revolution and equally necessary in the Civil War.

Ingersoll's precise and detailed citations of precedent included quotations from letters, documents, and the proceedings of the Continental Congress, and he demonstrated that, on the stump as in the courtroom, he appeared only after thorough preparation. Nevertheless, he invariably took advantage of each opportunity to link Tories and Democrats. The resulting implications are clear: the Republicans were the direct heirs of the revolutionary tradition and protectors of the constitutional realm. The Democrats, conversely, had inherited the mantle of those who denied and who would have destroyed American government and traditions. The "bloody shirt," less emotional but no less real than its use by Republican orators for the next generation, was evident, as it was to continue to be in Ingersoll's campaign oratory.

The second charge, that of freeing, arming, and enfranchising the Negro, engendered blunt defiance as well as support in precedent: "What next do they charge against us? That we freed negroes. So we did. That we allowed those negroes to fight in the army. Yes, we did. That we allowed them to vote. We did that too. That we have made them citizens. Yes, we have, and what are you Democrats going to do about it? " (IX, 39).

Again Ingersoll marshaled his evidence to support the action through precedent. For Ingersoll as for Lincoln, the Republican party was not radical in seeking to alter the values and structures of the country but conservative; it sought to preserve and defend them. Ingersoll cited the record of Negroes in the Revolution, emphasizing Crispus Attucks and the Boston Massacre, the raising of Negro troops, and the resulting freedom and franchise extended to them in many of the states. In this instance, documentation was sketchy; but Ingersoll compensated for that lack by presenting a document that provided the authorization for the raising, freeing, and rewarding of Negro troops. Actually, however, what Ingersoll made to appear to be a Civil War document was not. As he read it, it was made to appear through innuendo and careful juxtaposing of names to be an appeal issued by General Benjamin Butler to Negroes in Louisiana, calling for volunteers and citing their roles and responsibilities as citizens. This, Ingersoll says, is a terrible document to a Democrat—again implying that all rebels were Democrats—as he turns back to a careful examination of its phraseology: references to Negroes as Americans, to their intelligence, to their sense of honor, and to the rewards in bounties and land, the same as for whites, to which they are entitled. "Is not this a vile abolition document?" he inquires. "And yet there is not a Democrat in Indiana that dare open his mouth against it, full of negro equality as it is" (IX, 44).

The reason for this inability becomes clear as Ingersoll points out its origin, an origin presumably incomprehensible to Democrats:

> Now let us see when and by whom this proclamation was issued. You will find that it is dated "Headquarters 7th Military District, Mobile, September 21st, 1814," and signed "Andrew Jackson, Major General Commanding."
>
> Oh, you Jackson Democrats. You gentlemen that are descended from Washington and Jackson—great heavens, what a descent! He generally passed for a good Democrat; yet he issued that abominable abolition proclamation and put negroes on an equality with white men. . . . (IX, 44–45)

After skillfully depriving the Democrats of their patron saint by gathering Andrew Jackson into the Abolition fold, Ingersoll reiterated, as though he were marshaling evidence for the defense, the evidence he had presented. Then, as in his final addresses to the jury in criminal cases, he turned to the emotional, indicting not only Democrats but all Americans for the crime of slavery before the Civil War but the Democrats alone for its continuation in "the dominion of the Democrat, the bloodhound, and the lash" (IX, 49). As a final blow, he implied that the Democrats were cowards and hypocrites; that, when the draft came and they were threatened by military service, they were eager to have Negroes serve in their places.

The rest of the speech was an anticlimax. In deference to the specific demands of the occasion, Ingersoll turned briefly to Republican plans for Reconstruction and for reducing the national debt, attacking in passing the record of Horatio Seymour, the Democratic candidate, before concluding with a eulogy of the character, ability, and courage of General Grant.

As the first of Ingersoll's political speeches to receive nationwide attention, it provided the basis for his emerging reputation as one of the most effective stump speakers the Republican regulars had at their command. The remarkably objective account of the occasion and of the speech in the Indianapolis *Journal* for September 23, 1868, testifies to its effectiveness in arousing what was admittedly a partisan audience. Especially noticeable, the account concluded, were the abilities he used so effectively:

Colonel Ingersoll spoke at a great disadvantage in having so large a hall to fill, but he has a splendid voice and so overcame the difficulty. The audience liberally applauded the numerous passages of eloquence and humor in Colonel Ingersoll's speech, and listened with the best attention to his powerful argument, nor could they have done otherwise, for the speaker has a national reputation and did himself full justice last night.[1]

Although invariably Ingersoll's public projection of the image of the Republican party was virtue personified, he recognized clearly that his party had its quota of scoundrels, about whom he was not reluctant to comment in private. As in his private attitude toward the law, he was skeptical, if not contemptuous, of politicians in general, particularly of those in power, regardless of party. His comments to his brother John about the nature of the legislative process are indicative of his general attitude toward that profession he had once aspired to join and to which he gave much support: "I was at Springfield several weeks during the sitting of the Legislature and I suppose a more scaly set of one-horse thieves and low lived political tricksters never assembled on the earth. The thing called law I am daily losing respect for, and I think that Congress is but little better than our own Legislature. . . ."[2]

Nevertheless, Ingersoll's antipathy toward politics was less deeply felt than his attitude toward the law. In both cases the structure and the ideology upon which it is based were not at fault; rather, it was the conversion by men of that structure and ideology into workable reality that provided the opportunity for corruption at worst and failure to achieve the ideal at best. Even in Ingersoll's optimism about the Grant campaign and before the failure of his own nomination for the governorship in 1868, he was conscious of the imminent failure of a system based upon ideals but dependent upon men for its execution:

. . . we will have plenty to do to get the party of God and Humanity through the wilderness. It may be that we will elect Grant. That will likely be our last victory for years. I think the beloved country, "The best government the sun ever shone on etc" is very nearly on its last legs.

The same old story is being repeated. A people by revolution creates a nation. The nation cemented by blood—upheld by patriotism, common glory, common danger, becomes an empire. The people become wealthy—private individuals surpass offices of the government not only in wealth and ability but in the public estimation. Authority gets shabby. Rebellion rises. Debt is created. A tax gatherer at every door. Law becomes odious. The Government becomes despotic because it requires despotism to execute odious laws. And then as it says in the Almanac "About this time look out for stormy weather. . . ." [3]

II *The Campaign of 1872*

Although Ingersoll, after having spoken for Grant in Maine as well as in Indiana, was delighted with Grant's comfortable margin of victory in the election, he was nevertheless apprehensive about the future of the party without Andrew Johnson as a convenient scapegoat. Perhaps because of an innate suspicion of Grant's presidential abilities and undoubtedly because of his decision to withdraw from political candidacy and the increasing demands of the law practice and lecturing, Ingersoll took almost no active part in the fortunes of his party until 1876. By 1872, he determined to have no more to do with campaign speaking despite his disenchantment with Grant and his desire to see a change in the White House. To Jesse W. Fell, Republican leader and friend of Lincoln, he made this attitude clear:

I can conceive of no circumstances under which I would make a political speech. If ever in this world a man was thoroughly sick of political speaking, I am that man. Understand me, I am an admirer and friend of Judge Davis. I want to see him President of the United States and I believe he will be. And what little I do will be done for him. I am going to take no active part for anybody. For some reason, the leaders in politics are not my friends, and never have been. My only ambition is to get a living and to take good care of my family. . . .[4]

Although Judge David Davis failed to capture the regular Republican nomination from Grant and subsequently ran as the candidate of the Labor Reform party and the Liberal Republicans, Ingersoll remained true to his word for another four years. The source of his determination to remain aloof was undoubtedly his disappointment in Illinois and his conviction that he had been sold out by the Republican leadership. It also appears that he had doubts about "the party of God and Humanity" except in the most ironic sense when Grant received a renewed mandate to govern and when much of the party leadership regarded that mandate as popular approval of the alliances they had contracted and of the mutual benefit societies they had established. In 1875, Ingersoll wrote to Leonard Swett, another of Lincoln's old friends who tried to maintain the old Republican faith, that that faith must be re-established:

Unless the future is to be governed by the principle that none are beneath or above the law our race is a failure.

If we are to be bound hand and foot by one or the other of the corpses called parties; or if we are to surrender to conventions and resolutions all our political convictions; if we are to follow the chariot of some manufactured leader; if we are to grace the triumph of accident, cunning and ignorance, and if this is the whole political duty of man, the sooner this nation dies and rots, the better.

As long as it can be said of a people, of a government, that they who do the least have the most; that cunning idleness eats the bread of honest industry; that the rich grow richer and the poor poorer—that social differences continually increase, and that the consumers consume the producers—such a government—no matter what may be its name or form is an unmitigated shame and curse.[5]

III *The Campaign of 1876*

Nevertheless, just one year later Ingersoll was back in the active political arena. Trembling, he said later, for the future of Negroes in America if a Democratic president were elected, he became, as a result of his appearance at the Republican National Convention, one of the most noted and most popular speakers in the party as well as one of its most active. Gone were the doubts, the contempt, the near-despair, and he emerged an important Republican publically and as a devout Republican privately. The party had once more become the party of freedom—or at least he convinced himself that it had.

The reasons for this dramatic shift are difficult to determine, but the fact that Ingersoll's chosen candidate, James G. Blaine, enjoyed a reputation less than spotless suggests a reason less than ideological for Ingersoll's re-emergence on the stump. Blaine's drive for the nomination was hampered by the fact that the so-called Mulligan letters revealed his connection with the Fort Worth and Little Rock Railroad as less than honorable. As Speaker of the House in 1869, he had saved the railroad's land grant and had subsequently sold bonds for it on commission. Although the scandal never fully emerged, and although specific details about the extent of Blaine's involvement are scanty, rumors and innuendoes were rife, to the detriment of his chances for the presidential nomination. The support of Illinois, a key state, was crucial; and Blaine's Illinois representative, Congressman Stephen A. Hurlbut, suggested that Ingersoll place Blaine's name in nomination. The idea intrigued Blaine and attracted Ingersoll. On June 15, 1876, he arose in the convention hall in Cincinnati to deliver one of the most noted nominating speeches in the history of the American convention system; and he followed it by devoting his full energies and talents to the election of his party's nominee because, as he later insisted, the rights of free Americans were in danger in the South. There is also evidence, however, to suggest that he was attracted, at least momentarily, by the possibility of his being appointed to a diplomatic post abroad.

The nomination speech itself was one of the briefest political speeches Ingersoll ever delivered, despite its also being the most celebrated. Following the nomination speech for Benjamin A. Bristow—Grant's secretary of the treasury and a liberal, honest man who not only remained true but inhibited some of the activities of those who misunderstood the nature of Grant's mandate—Ingersoll opened his speech with a paragraph designed to deflate Bristow's appeal and to enhance Blaine's:

> Massachusetts may be satisfied with the loyalty of Benjamin H. Bristow; so am I; but if any man nominated by this convention can not carry the State of Massachusetts, I am not satisfied with the loyalty of that State. If the nominee of this convention cannot carry the grand old Commonwealth of Massachusetts by seventy-five thousand majority, I would advise them to sell out Faneuil Hall as a Democratic headquarters. I would advise them to take from Bunker Hill that old monument of glory. (IX, 55)

But the question of Massachusetts' loyalty was not important, and Ingersoll knew it. The crucial issue for his candidate's chances was his reputation, and Ingersoll devoted the rest of his speech to its refurbishment. In the tradition of nominating speeches, he first defined the qualities demanded by the nation, the party, and the hour, qualities which, it was evident, his candidate possessed: a statesman, a reformer, a man of known opinions, a man versed in domestic and international affairs, "a politican in the highest, broadest and best sense—a man of superb moral courage," a man of impeccably conservative financial bent, and, of most importance, "a man whose political reputation is spotless as a star." There was obviously only one man, he insisted, having all those necessary qualifications: "The man who has, in full, heaped and rounded measure, is the present grand and gallant leader of the Republican Party—James G. Blaine."

But the most quoted part of the speech, at once a magnificent tribute and a poignant plea, was yet to come:

Like an armed warrior, like a plumed knight, James G. Blaine marched down the halls of the American Congress and threw his shining lance full and fair against the brazen foreheads of the defamers of his country and the maligners of his honor. For the Republicans party to desert this gallant leader now, is as though an army should desert their general upon the field of battle.

James G. Blaine is now and has been for years the bearer of the sacred standard of the Republican party. I call it sacred, because no human being can stand beneath its folds without becoming and without remaining free.

Gentlemen of the convention, in the name of the Republic, the only republic that ever existed upon this earth; in the name of all her defenders and of all her supporters; in the name of all her soldiers living; in the name of all her soldiers dead upon the field of battle, and in the name of all those who perished in the skeleton clutch of famine at Andersonville and Libby, whose sufferings he so vividly remembers, Illinois—Illinois nominates for the next President of this country, that prince of parliamentarians—that leader of leaders—James G. Blaine. (IX, 59–60)

With the sacred standard of the Republican party unfurled to reveal it as the "bloody shirt," Ingersoll made his nominating speech the tour de force of the convention. Blaine's detractors were those who would see the party and its strongest, most able champion destroyed; for his motives were pure, his reputation unsullied, his virtue unblemished in the eyes of patriotic men everywhere, and his unmatched qualifications were presented for appraisal. As in Ingersoll's arguments as defense attorney, he turned the accusations against his accusers; the result, as he pointed out, could be only one decision.

The reception of the speech in the convention hall was as Ingersoll anticipated; if a nomination by acclamation of the crowd were possible at that point, the conclusion would have been foregone. As the correspondent of the Chicago *Tribune* described the scene, however, the man of the hour was not Blaine but Ingersoll:

Possessed of a fine figure, a face of winning, cordial frankness, Ingersoll had half won his audience before he spoke a word. It is the attestation of every man that heard him, that so brilliant a master stroke was never uttered before a political Convention. Its effect was indescribable. The coolest-headed in the hall were stirred to the wildest expression. . . . The matchless method and manner of the man can never be imagined from the report in type. . . .

Words can do but meagre justice to the wizard power of this
extraordinary man. He swayed and moved and impelled and restrained
and worked in all ways with the mass before him as if he possessed
some key to the innermost mechanism that moves the human heart,
and when he finished, his fine, frank face as calm as when he began, the
overwrought thousands sank back in an exhaustion of unspeakable
wonder and delight.[6]

Although Ingersoll's plan was not only to refurbish Blaine's
reputation but to sweep the convention on a wave of sentimentality—
and he came close to accomplishing both—he did not succeed. The
combination of Blaine's reputation, political enemies, and a shrewd
move by the convention leaders to adjourn to the next morning—
ostensibly because of unsafe gas lights but in reality to allow the
atmosphere of Ingersoll's speech to dissipate—combined to frustrate the
plans of the Blaine forces. The critics commented that an honest Blaine
is the noblest work of Bob. The next day the convention became
lackluster; the nominee, Rutherford B. Hayes of Ohio—a war veteran,
brevetted general, safe, impeccably honest, and a dark horse—matched
the air of the convention.

In spite of Ingersoll's candidate's loss, he was persuaded to take to
the stump, and he did so throughout the Northeast. Perhaps he had
visions once more of a political career, but he more likely began to
enjoy one vicariously and to recognize the importance of his role as
king-maker. Without question, he was the most popular Republican
orator in the field; and the ultimate effect of his speeches upon the
electorate, while impossible to measure, was undoubtedly of great value
in view of the extremely close margin of votes between Hayes and his
Democratic opponent, Samuel J. Tilden of New York.

The election marked the one-hundredth anniversary of American
independence, and Ingersoll, dubbed the "Centennial Spread Eagle" of
the Republican party, used that fact to the utmost because, as he later
insisted, he believed that a Democratic victory would mean the end of
American freedom and democracy. He spoke to crowds of tens of
thousands wherever he went, and the effect was as spontaneously
explosive as it had been in the convention hall. His critics and some
friends, including Chauncey Depew, insisted that he delivered one
speech many times rather than a series of speeches, and there is much
substance to the statement. In each case, the substance was the same,
but circumstances often altered specifics. Depew commented that in
each case Ingersoll swept his audience off its feet; Depew also remarked

in wonder that each day the speech was printed in full in the newspapers as though it had been entirely new.

In each speech Ingersoll made his case for the Republicans and damned the Democrats, and in each he waved the "bloody shirt" with vigor. In tracing the history of the country, he made it clear that God, Country, and Republicanism were synonymous, as were the devil, treason, and the Democrats. But most important, both as a new idea for Ingersoll and as a note of substance within the campaign oratory, is a firm stand in favor of economic conservatism and specifically for the redemption of greenbacks in gold. In his speech at the Cooper Union on September 10, he developed his case for gold redemption and a sound, deflated dollar with conservative patriotic logic:

> The people have to support the Government; the Government cannot support the people. The Government has no money but what it received from the people. It therefore had to borrow money to carry on the war. Every greenback that it issued was a forced loan. My notes are not a legal tender. . . . The alchemists in olden times who fancied that they could make gold out of nothing were not more absurd than the American advocates of soft money.
>
> . . . Gold is the best material which labor has yet found as a measure of value. That object of value must be as valuable as the object it measures.
>
> The value of gold arises from the amount of labor expended in producing it. A gold dollar will buy as much labor as produced that dollar. . . . (IX, 147–49)

But Ingersoll did not dwell upon this elementary lesson in conservative economics; after asserting that Republicans intended to pay their debts in gold, he returned to his indictment of the Democratic party as one of thieves and to his attack on Tilden personally by using the innuendo that "I understand that . . ." both were sympathizers with treason and slavery. "Tammany Hall," he insisted, "bears the same relationship to the penitentiary that the Sunday school does to the church."

On this occasion, as on others, Ingersoll felt it necessary to deflect some of the critical barbs aimed at his agnosticism; and he did so skillfully, again raising the issue through innuendo and disarming it so simply that either sympathizer or critic could make of his statement what he would: "I want every schoolhouse to be a temple of science in which shall be taught the laws of nature, in which children shall be taught actual facts, and I do not want that schoolhouse touched, or that institution of science touched, by any superstition whatever. Leave religion with the church, with the family, and more than all, leave religion with each individual heart and man . . ." (IX, 153–54).

In each manifestation of his speech, Ingersoll maintained a strong offensive against the Democrats, obviously because it was the only tactic that promised success. The actual record of Republican administrations under Grant would not bear inspection, and Hayes had neither record nor reputation to extoll; consequently, the major issue which the Republicans could raise was that of equating the Democrats with treason. But Ingersoll did not hesitate to raise other issues; in his Chicago speech, he turned devastating wit and innuendo again on Tilden personally:

I am opposed to him, first, because he is an old bachelor. In a country like ours, depending for its prosperity and glory upon an increase of the population, to elect an old bachelor is a suicidal policy. Any man that will live in this country for sixty years, surrounded by beautiful women with rosy lips and dimpled cheeks, in every dimple lurking a Cupid, with pearly teeth and sparkling eyes—any man that will push them all aside and be satisfied with the embraces of the Democratic party, does not even know the value of time. . . . (IX, 209)

This version, edited from the newspapers accounts, conveys the innuendo clearly enough; the laughter, snickers, and shouts as references to a "little, dried-up old bachelor" were interspersed, making Ingersoll's comments devastating.

The Indianapolis speech, delivered before a gathering of Civil War veterans and designed to make them the arm of the Republican party they became, was noted for two elements: the bluntest accusations against the Democrats in the entire campaign and the passage that became known and revered as Ingersoll's "Vision of War." Ingersoll, "that dashing cavalry officer, that thunderbolt of war, that silver-tongued orator," as General Noyes called him in his introduction, leaped immediately to the attack:

I am opposed to the Democratic party, and I will tell you why. Every State that seceded from the United States was a Democratic State. Every ordinance of secession that was drawn was drawn by a Democrat. Every man that endeavored to tear the old flag from the heaven that it enriches was a Democrat. Every enemy this great Republic has had for twenty years has been a Democrat. Every man that shot Union soldiers was a Democrat. Every man that denied to the Union prisoners even the worm-eaten crust of famine, and when some poor, emaciated Union patriot, driven to insanity by famine, saw in an insane dream the face of his mother, and she beckoned him and he followed, hoping to press her lips once again against his fevered face, and when he stepped one step beyond the dead line, the wretch that put the bullet through his loving, throbbing heart was and is a Democrat.

... The man that assassinated Abraham Lincoln was a Democrat.... Every man that raised bloodhounds to pursue human beings was a Democrat.... Soldiers, every scar you have on your heroic bodies was given you by a Democrat.... (IX, 157—60)

The fact that these and the dozens of other accusations were simply neither true nor relevant was immaterial to the partisan audience, and Ingersoll raised its emotions to an intense pitch before citing the reasons he was a Republican. Again he equated Republicanism with the American virtues, to the glee of his audience, who were, at this point, reminded that they had been soldiers. As a sudden rainstorm swept over the field, the general shouted, "What is rain to soldiers? " The audience roared to continue, and Ingersoll went on eulogizing his party and equating the heroism of his audience and party: "And right here I want to thank every soldier that fought to make [the country] free, every one living and dead. I thank you again and again and again. You made the first free government in the world, and we must not forget the dead heroes. If they were here they would vote the Republican ticket, every one of them. I tell you we must not forget them" (IX, 166—67).

From this point, actually jarring in the context of what had gone before and what was to come later, Ingersoll began the passage called "A Vision of War." A flight of sentimental fancy, obviously designed to reawaken memories that his audience, his candidate, and he himself had shared, it provided the rationale, just as the pension bills provided the substance, for the strong alliance between the Grand Old Party and the Grand Army of the Republic:

The past rises before me like a dream. Again we are in the great struggle for national life. We hear the sounds of preparation—the music of boisterous drums—the silver voices of heroic bugles. ... We see them part with those they love. ... We see them as they march proudly away. ... We are by their side on all the glory fields—in all the hospitals of pain—on all the weary marches. ...

The past rises before us. We hear the roar and shriek of the bursting shell. The broken fetters fall. These heroes died. We look. Instead of slaves we see men and women. ...

The heroes are dead. . . . In the midst of battle, in the roar of conflict, they found the serenity of death. I have one sentiment for soldiers living and dead: cheers for the living, tears for the dead. (IX, 167–70)

At this point, Ingersoll returned to the substance of his speech: the necessity for redeeming greenbacks in gold and the continued damnation of the Democrats. In the final lines, he saw a vision of the future, a Republican future made meaningful through the leadership of virtue and wisdom.

Ingersoll continued to speak to the end of the campaign, thus making himself a national celebrity and a lecturer so much in demand that he was forced to employ a clerk to keep the requests straight. Later, he became the most popular lecturer in James Redpath's Lyceum Bureau. In both cases, his popularity was paradoxical because at the same time he engendered much personal antagonism, some of it satirical but much completely serious. To one editor, it was unfortunate that Ingersoll could not lead the party faithful in prayer; to another, it appeared that Fort Sumter was under fire once more. To others, accepting the support of a notorious atheist was calling down the judgment of God on the party and on the candidate.

Indeed, as the election passed and remained in doubt because of disputed votes, it seemed to some that God was displeased as the centennial election became a mockery of the democratic ideal. Although Tilden received a majority of the popular vote, with 184 certain electoral votes, and although Hayes had a certain total of 165, with 185 necessary for election, 20 electoral votes from Oregon, Florida, Louisiana, and South Carolina were in dispute. In the last three states, the governments were in Democratic hands and the election machinery in Republican. With no constitutional means for settling the dispute, Congress appointed a special Electoral Commission composed of five senators, five representatives, and five Supreme Court justices. The resulting vote, divided eight to seven on party lines, gave the disputed votes to Hayes, thereby electing him by one electoral vote. The resulting threat to national unity from dissident Democrats was settled by the agreement whereby the Democrats would not contest the election if federal troops were withdrawn from southern occupation. The agreement thus paved the way for the continued powerful coalition of Republicans and southern Democrats, to the advantage of the new industrialism and to the disadvantage of Negroes whom the Republicans had presumably championed for a generation.

The shoddiness of the campaign and its aftermath was reflected from the very beginning in Ingersoll's speeches, a collection of documents that continue to be embarrassing to his apologists. Almost devoid of substance, of political philosophy, of objective evidence, or of party programs, their intent was without question to hinder rather than enhance rational discussion of the issues. Although such attempts are far from unknown in the American political tradition, particularly in the West where Ingersoll grew up, Ingersoll's apologists have nevertheless found them difficult to account for. Almost invariably they are seen as momentary lapses in the heat of a political campaign or they are interpreted as conveying a genuine hatred of slavery and opposition to all its manifestations.

But slavery had been dead for a decade; the Negro had been enfranchised by federal law and bayonets; and the pressing issues of the moment were not of the past but of the present and future—social, economic, and political, including advancement for the race that Ingersoll had championed. In his "one speech" he did insist upon gold redemption for greenbacks, a cause which he equated with patriotism, but that was all; the great issues were forgotten by a party and by a spokesman dedicated to freedom. His championship of the Negro was well known and publicized, especially in incidents of his own kindness and charity, but in his major opportunity to influence the course of the future for that race, he either did not see, or chose not to seize, the opportunity.

Two possibilities for Ingersoll's role in this campaign suggest themselves. The first and undoubtedly the most probable in the light of his skepticism toward politics and the law is that he regarded politics as a game and as a business rather than as a matter of competing political philosophies; and, carried away by the power of the persuasive orator who could mould and move crowds by the exercise of his eloquence, he did so with all the effectiveness at his command. The other is that Ingersoll still had political hopes or ambitions, as suggested by a provocative letter to his family, written as late as eight months after the Hayes adminstration took office. Friends had recommended him for a diplomatic mission abroad; and, when it had not materialized—and there is no evidence to suggest that he sought it directly in spite of his services in the campaign, surely deserving of some reward—he wrote, with an air of martyrdom: "You need place no confidence in what you hear about the Berlin mission—I do not believe that Hayes dare appoint me. He is afraid of the religious world. I must be and I am perfectly willing to pay for the privilege of saying what I think. I shall not call on the President until my return from Utica, Syracuse and Albany, and shall not then say a word about Berlin. . . .[7] "

Nevertheless, Ingersoll's Republican faith was strained after the inauguration for other reasons. A conservative and formerly a Radical Republican, Ingersoll found Hayes' policy of reconciling the South dangerous, and he began to think that perhaps Tilden would have been a better choice, even that perhaps he had indeed been elected. Part of this reaction was undoubtedly due to personal disappointment, perhaps pique at Hayes' unwillingness to reward him for his services in the face of newspaper and religious hostility; but rationally he must have known that the rumored Cabinet post and the recommended diplomatic post would not have been forthcoming from the conservative Methodist Hayes and his wife, the "Lemonade Lucy" of fact and folklore.

In 1879, Ingersoll began to think about the formation of a third political party, in conjunction with Thaddeus Burr Wakeman, a friend and leading Freethinker. The basic principles of the projected new party, as Ingersoll saw it, were essentially those of the separation of church and state rather than the more conventional social, economic, or political principles. He wrote:

. . . I am willing to help organize a new political party based: First, upon the utter divorce of Church and State. Second, a divorce of Church and School. Third, the taxation of all private property. Fourth, the repeal of all laws abridging work for one day in the week—the rights of the citizen, and of the laws denying to any man any civil right on account of his belief or unbelief.

I believe we can succeed in a far shorter time by Federal than by State action. I am not willing to join for any purpose whatever, the present Democratic party, nor to act with it. I am not willing to join the Greenback party, nor to act with it for any purpose whatever. I am willing to help organize a new party, and to allow any and everybody to act with us.[8]

IV *The Campaign of 1880*

Ingersoll's plan for a third party, like countless others, came to nothing, and Ingersoll remained in the Republican party, although his roles in future campaigns never again approached the extent or power of his activities in 1876. In the convention of 1880, he had no part, although he made clear his displeasure with Hayes and with John Sherman. Blaine and Grant, seeking a third term, emerged as the major contenders, but the ultimate nominee was James A. Garfield, who, like

Hayes, was a former Civil War general, a religious man, and a dark horse from Ohio. Although Ingersoll immediately joined the Garfield forces, the Democratic nominee, Winfield S. Hancock, another Civil War general and an authentic hero at Gettysburg, was such that the "bloody shirt" tactics of 1876 simply would not work in 1880.

Ingersoll spoke frequently again, starting with Maine at the behest of Blaine, and covering a circuit between there and Illinois. Although he continued to denounce the Democrats, his accusations were less intense and a great deal milder. Even the Republican party was sometimes less than perfect, he asserted with an air of great candor; and the Democratic party had, on rare occasions, done the right thing. But the Republican party and its unblemished candidate, James A. Garfield, were incomparably the best.

However, much critical irony was directed at the unexplained role of Garfield in the Crédit Mobilier scandal and at the spectacle of Ingersoll speaking for a man who remained a lay preacher in the Disciples of Christ Church. But the course of the campaign saw a strong alliance between Ingersoll the agnostic and the Republican clergy, especially with Henry Ward Beecher. With Beecher, he began a warm friendship that itself became the subject of a great deal of humor, particularly when they occupied the same platform. During the campaign, Ingersoll and Garfield also became close friends; but there is nothing to suggest that Ingersoll had either political ambitions or hopes in 1880.

If Ingersoll's speeches in 1880 were milder, they were no less devoid of political philosophy or of economic or social principles. Although he had publicly advocated civil service reform in 1877 and the extension of the franchise to residents of the District of Columbia earlier in 1880, there were no such suggestions in his speeches, most of which were, as in 1876, one speech. Nevertheless, on several occasions Ingersoll found it necessary to depart from the rhetorical generalities of party praise and to turn his attention to immediate criticism of his role in the party, the alliance between himself and the clergy, and the continued rumors about the character of his candidate. His attacks on Hancock were mild in comparison with the rigor of his defense.

On one such occasion, in Brooklyn on October 30, after being introduced by Henry Ward Beecher, he found it necessary to refute all these problems. After his rhetorical praise of patriotism, party, and nation, he attacked Hancock on the tariff, on southern pensions and claims, and on ex-Confederates in public office. In each case, he maintained, Hancock was attempting to disassociate himself from the party; but the party, not Hancock, would make policy. Then he turned to a vigorous, aggressive defense: "They tell me that James A. Garfield is not honest. Are you a Democrat? Your party tried to steal nearly half of this country. Your party stole the armament of a nation. Your party was willing to live upon the unpaid labor of four millions of people . . ." (IX, 397).

From the defense of Garfield he turned then to his own as well:

> I know Garfield—I like him. Some people have said, "How is it that you support Garfield, when he was a minister? " "How is it that you support Garfield when he is a Christian? " I will tell you. There are two reasons. The first is I am not a bigot; and secondly, James A. Garfield is not a bigot. He believes in giving to every other human being every right he claims for himself. . . . He disagrees with me in many things; but in the one thing, that the air is free for all, we do agree. I want to do equal and exact justice everywhere . . . . (IX, 399—400)

Ingersoll turned then to the presence of Henry Ward Beecher on the same platform. Beecher, a firm admirer of Ingersoll's oratorical talents—in introducting Ingersoll on that occasion, he referred to him as "the most brilliant speaker of the English tongue of all men on this globe"—was well aware of the dangerous implications of their sharing the same platform, as was Ingersoll; and he had in his introduction allayed some of the doubts about the alliance. Now it was Ingersoll's turn:

> I want the world to be without a chain, without a wall, and I wish to say to you [turning toward Mr. Beecher and directly addressing him] that I thank you for what you have said tonight, and to congratulate the people of this city and country that you have intellectual horizon enough, intellectual sky enough to take the hand of a man, howsoever much he may disagree in some things with you, on the grand platform and broad principles of citizenship. James A. Garfield, believing with me as he does, disagreeing with me as he does, is perfectly satisfactory to me. I know him, and I like him. (IX, 400)

After denying the rumors of an unholy, cynical alliance for dishonest purposes, Ingersoll turned quickly again to denying the charges against Garfield's honesty: "Men are today blackening his reputation, who are not fit to blacken his shoes. . . . Lie after lie has been told about him. Slander after slander has been hatched and put in the air, with its little short wings, to fly its day, and the last lie is a forgery" (IX, 400—401). The continued refutations without evidence but with the force of rhetoric, of emotional assertion, and of what appeared to be deep but simple candor proved an effective political platform, and the campaign ended with Garfield's election.

Although a close personal friendship continued between Ingersoll, Garfield, and Mrs. Lucretia Garfield, suggesting the possibility of Ingersoll's strong influence on the coming administration, the relationship did not last. Shot by Charles Guiteau on July, 2, 1881, Garfield died on September 19. His successor, Chester A. Arthur, a Republican regular about whom rumors were rife, was not friendly to Ingersoll; and Ingersoll's entry to the White House circle vanished as quickly as it had come about. Nevertheless, as Garfield lay dying, rumors about the shooting began to circulate. Americans found it impossible to accept the assassination of a president as the result of anything other than a gigantic and powerful conspiracy. Ingersoll was quick to deny the rumors and to defend Arthur and Roscoe Conkling, who were cast as the villains:

... Of course you have read all about the affair in the papers. I get news from the White House every few minutes. We have been so stretched and strained on the rack of hope and fear that we are all worn out. ... All the stuff in the papers about Conspiracy is stuff and nothing else. All the charges that Conkling and Arthur are responsible are too absurd to be talked about.

Guiteau, the murderer, wanted an office. The President was troubled by him—ordered him to keep away—told the servants not to admit him. Guiteau became malicious and shot the President. That is all there is about it. The crime has no political significance. It is humiliating to read the follies of the press and pulpit on this matter. . . . [9]

Although Charles Guiteau, a religious fanatic as well as a disappointed office seeker, had publicly attacked Ingersoll in the past and had predicted a tragic, fearful end for the unbeliever, Ingersoll chose not to comment. The assassination, with its rumors and relationships, contained within itself the substance of folklore and invective. But the books of history have fortunately closed upon the matter, and under Arthur, a surprisingly honest and conscientious president, the life of the country went on, marked by the progress of civil service reform.

V *The Campaign of 1884*

The election of 1880 was Ingersoll's last major political effort, perhaps because of the strained relations that developed between him

and his former "plumed knight," James G. Blaine. In 1884, when
Blaine was the nominee, Ingersoll did not make a single campaign
speech, and the reasons for the break between them have never been
made clear. Although Ingersoll had preferred as the nominee either
John Harland of Kentucky or Walter Gresham of Indiana, he seemed
willing enough to support Blaine, although he commented that he could
see no important issues in the campaign and preferred at the time to
fight the church rather than the Democrats. Various reasons have been
ascribed to the break: a quarrel between Mrs. Blaine and Mrs. Ingersoll;
the failure of Ingersoll's friends to receive offices under Garfield as a
result of Blaine's opposition from within the cabinet as Secretary of
State; Blaine's unwillingness to have Ingersoll's support because of his
reputation as an agnostic and because of his role in the *Star Route*
trials. The evidence does suggest, however, that the *Star Route* trials
were a major cause of the never healed wound between them; and in
1888 Ingersoll deliberately praised the honesty of Roscoe Conkling,
Blaine's old enemy, to the embarrassment of Blaine. The evidence also
suggests that had Blaine been willing, the rupture might have been
healed easily. As the returns came in in 1884, Ingersoll wrote:

> I am just a little glad that New York is so close.—I feel way down in
> my gaiters that I could have carried that state for Blaine, and it occurs
> to me that Blaine will have a like suspicion in his mind.—Of course it is
> wrong to be a little malicious, but I am growing that way as I grow
> older. Blaine has reached the end of his career. I sometimes wish that he
> had allowed me to be his friend—in other words—I regret that he is not
> the man I once thought he was. . . .[10]

In 1886, Ingersoll departed briefly from his Republican faith to
support Henry George for mayor of New York on the single-tax ticket.
Intrigued by the idea of the single tax and disenchanted with the
Republicans even to the extent that he said kind—or at least not
unkind—words about the Cleveland administration, he did little in
direct support of George, primarily because of a throat ailment, but he
wrote letters and gave interviews in which he made clear his support.
Although George was defeated by the Democrat, Abram S. Hewitt, he
outran Theodore Roosevelt; and Ingersoll suggested that, had Roosevelt
and the Republicans withdrawn, as he was convinced they should have
done, the city and ultimately the country would have been the better
for it.

VI *The Campaign of 1888*

Economically conservative as well as economically innocent, Ingersoll knew little of the nature of finance or investment—he lost heavily on a number of occasions—and he turned quickly back to the Republican orthodox insistence upon sound money based upon gold and a high protective tariff. In 1888, he attended the Republican national convention as a supporter of Gresham and perhaps inadvertently precipitated an unscheduled, unplanned demonstration. Prevailed upon by cheers of the crowd, he began to speak, giving in essence what had become his standard eulogy of the Republican party. But in the midst, he declaimed, "Feeling so, I am in favor of the nomination of Judge Walter Q. Gresham."

At that, Gresham's supporters began a massive demonstration, suggesting that the remark was less than spontaneous and that the Gresham forces and Ingersoll, remembering the near-nomination by acclamation of Blaine in 1876, had planned to seize control of the convention. But a near-riot ensued as partisans began to battle one another, using banners and signs as weapons. Finally, however, a man with a powerful voice was brought to the platform; and he began to read. Unintelligible at first, he finally began to he heard; he was reading Thomas Buchanan Read's poem, "Sheridan's Ride." Silence fell over the hall, for the men of the convention knew that Sheridan was dying at that moment, and they quietly and respectfully adjourned the convention.

Ingersoll's attitude toward Benjamin Harrison, the nominee, was at best lukewarm; but Harrison was orthodox on the tariff issue, the major one of the campaign, and he also opposed Cleveland's war record and his policy of conciliation toward the South. Although Ingersoll was suffering from a continued throat ailment, he spoke three times during the campaign, supporting the protective tariff and attacking Cleveland. But in acknowledging his continued admiration for Judge Gresham, he did Harrison no good. It is evident that there was something of the kingmaker in Ingersoll's attitude toward the presidential politics of his party.

Ingersoll's typical campaign speech of the year, delivered at the Metropolitan Opera House in New York on June 29, was far less emotional than those of the past and more directly focused upon the issues, in the discussion of which, however, he was willing to use emotional appeals. In many respects, Ingersoll came into political maturity in this campaign, undoubtedly because he had begun to recognize the reality of party allegiance. The ties were intellectual, social, and economic rather than personal, emotional, or historic, and he addressed his audience on that basis. The issue between the parties was clearly a case of economic alternatives, and he proceeded on that basis. The usual plea for Grand Army of the Republic support was included in the castigation of Cleveland's veto of the pension bill, but the bulk of the speech offered alternatives between what Ingersoll saw as good and as bad economics. He concluded, with an air of candor and disarming simplicity, that he was for the platform and, consequently, for the election of Benjamin Harrison.

Although Harrison won, Ingersoll had little to do with either the President or policy during the next four years; and in 1892, when Harrison and Cleveland faced each other again, Ingersoll did nothing for either the party or the candidate. He remarked that, although he would prefer to see the Republicans win and Harrison lose, that was impossible; therefore, he would vote for the party's candidate. But that was the extent of his party service in 1892.

VII *The Campaign of 1896*

In 1896, however, the situation was different. Although his health had deteriorated, Ingersoll was genuinely frightened by the upsurge of Populist sentiment in the 1890's and by the capture of the Democratic party by William Jennings Bryan and the forces of Free Silver. His belief in the necessity of a gold-based financial structure was an article of faith equaled only by his belief in the protective tariff; and McKinley, having proved his soundness on the latter issue, would, Ingersoll was certain, defend the former with vigor and success. Consequently, once more he embarked on a major speaking tour, focused primarily in the doubtful state of Illinois, although he also gave a major speech in New York. Actually, he again used the "one speech" technique; and, as in 1888, he focused upon the major issue rather than upon personalities or parties. In spite of McKinley's war record, for Ingersoll the "bloody shirt" had at last been laid to rest in his last political campaign. But he did not hesitate to castigate Bryan without mercy.

Ingersoll began with a lesson in elementary economics as taught by those who believed as he did:

What is a dollar? People imagine that a piece of paper with pictures on it, with signatures, is money. The greenback is not money—never was; never will be. It is a promise to pay money; not money. . . .

Well, what is a dollar? In the civilized world it is twenty-three grains
and twenty-two one hundredths of pure gold. That is a dollar . . . in
order to make a silver dollar you have got to put a dollar's worth of
silver in the silver dollar. . . . there is no way to make a dollar without
the value. (IX, 540—41)

It was this soundness that Bryan threatened and the mere threat made
him in Ingersoll's eyes the most dangerous man alive, much too
dangerous to be loose in the nation.

After examining Bryan's threat to a soundly high tariff, as well as a
sound dollar, and then insisting upon anti-lynching legislation, he
turned to Bryan:

. . . You have to choose between men. Shall Mr. Bryan be the next
President or shall McKinley occupy that chair? Who is Mr. Bryan? He is
not a tried man. If he had the capacity to reason, if he had logic, if he
could spread his wings of imagination, if there were in his heart the
divine flower called pity, he might be an orator, but lacking all these, he
is as he is.

While Major McKinley was fighting under the flag, Bryan was in his
mother's arms, and judging from his speeches he ought to be there still.
What is he? He is a Populist. He voted for General Weaver. Only a little
while ago he denied being a Democrat. His mind is filled with vagaries.
A fiat money man. His brain is an insane asylum without a keeper. . . .
(IX, 574—75)

Perhaps there was a bit of personal jealousy in this, Ingersoll's last
major political speech, delivered in New York. Again the question of his
agnosticism was raised before and after the speech, but the barbs were
humorously affectionate rather than filled with sharp invective.
Quotations of biblical origin were ascribed to him, such as that of the
New York *Journal*: "I want to see a dollar that can lift up its head and
say, 'My Redeemer liveth.' " In such jibes there was an air of nostalgia
that seemed to mark the passing of an era that would never come again.
Yet, although Ingersoll had aged, the fire and eloquence remained:

. . . The old warhorse, silvered by long years of faithful service to his
country, aroused the same all pervading enthusiasm as he did in the
campaigns of Grant and Hayes and Garfield.

He has lost not one whit, not one iota of his striking physical
presence, his profound reasoning, his convincing logic, his rollicking
wit, grandiloquence—in fine, all the graces of the orator of old,

reinforced by increased patriotism and ardor of the call to battle for his country, are still his in the fullest measure.

. . . Those passionate outbursts of eloquence, the wit that fairly scintillated, the logic as inexorable as heaven's decrees, his rich rhetoric and immutable facts driven straight to his hearers with the strength of bullets, aroused applause that came as spontaneous as sunlight. . . .[11]

With McKinley elected and the dollar apparently secured, at least for the time, Ingersoll caught some of the expansionist fever of the time. In fact, he had, as part of his patriotic fervor, always felt something of the sort. But, at the moment of the American empire realized, he had doubts about the justice as well as about the wisdom of the imperialist adventure that resulted from American victory in the Spanish-American War. In the last letter he was to write, written on July 20, 1899, the day before his death, he made clear his faith: that the American dream was free to all, but it was to be forced on none:

. . . It is true that I think the treatment of the Filipinos wrong— foolish. It is also true that I do not want the Flipinos if they do not want us. I believe in expansion—if it is honest.

I want Cuba if the Cubans want us.

At the same time, I think that our forces should be immediately withdrawn from Cuba, and the people of that island allowed to govern themselves. We waged the war against Spain for liberty—for right—and we must bear the laurel unstained.[12]

As a final comment on Ingersoll's long, active role in the political life of the country, this letter bears testimony to much of the force that motivated him. A magnificent spokesman for a party he had sustained with reasonable faithfulness for more than thirty years, he had used and abused his talents unstintingly, sometimes unscrupulously, in the significant campaigns of his time. There is no doubt that his influence in those campaigns was great and valuable to his party and its candidates, perhaps at times even decisive.

A conservative and patriot to the end, and a man with great faith in the democratic process, although he sometimes seemed to under-estimate the intelligence of the electorate, he was not a profound political thinker, nor was he versed in the great social and economic controversies of his day. Moreover, it is also possible to question the depths of his convictions about the men whom he sometimes supported so strongly. There is no evidence to suggest that, as he insisted, it was best to put ideas above party. Yet, in the final analysis, there is no doubt about his ultimate motive and his highest ideal. It was freedom that he wanted—not only for himself but for all men.

CHAPTER 4

"One world at a time is my doctrine . . ."

TO two generations of Americans, whether religiously orthodox or intellectually liberated to a greater or a lesser extent, the name Robert Ingersoll was synonymous with agnosticism at best and with atheism at worst. To the orthodox, he was responsible for the moral decay of post-Civil War America, for the increasing secularization of American society, and for the dissemination of ideas to seduce, ensnare, and destroy young people. To the liberated, he was a crusader for human freedom, an iconoclastic champion of science in its war against superstition, and a leader in man's long campaign to elevate himself above his primitive, animalistic origins. To the former, he was often the devil incarnate; to village Freethinkers across the length of America he was an example of man's potential realized. Neither faction could pretend indifference or ignore him.

Although there is much truth in both extreme positions, the truth in each is outweighed by the misinterpretations and misunderstandings as well as by the sheer fabrications that abound on each side. Ingersoll was not a pioneer or even an innovator in the Freethought or agnostic movements of the last half of the nineteenth century; he was a popularizer, and he never claimed to be more. At best, he was an adapter and synthesizer of other men's ideas; at worst, a mere parrot. Yet to dismiss him for lacking originality or to condemn him without acknowledging his contributions to the cause of free inquiry and humanistic concern would be to ignore what both extremes tacitly admit: that Robert Ingersoll occupies a central place in the intellectual, religious, and social controversies of his time. And the nature of that role was determined by the nature of the man; by his talents as an orator; and by his convictions about the nature of God, man, and the universe. In him, the rationalism of the eighteenth century and the Romantic faith in man of the nineteenth merged, and out of that merger derived Ingersoll's vision of progress and perfectibility that he articulated on countless lecture platforms. His prime purpose was to communicate that vision, but he also knew that he had to destroy before man could create—and all the evidence suggests that he found much, perhaps too much, joy in the destruction. He saw himself as an emancipator of the intellect just as his generation was the emancipator of men, and he marched roughshod over what he termed the slavery of superstitution just as relentlessly as Sherman's troops had marched through Georgia, destroying a civilization built by slavery and depending upon slavery for its continuance in power.

To Ingersoll, the parallel between the institution of human slavery and that of organized religion was real. The former enslaved men's bodies as it depended upon the fear of physical punishment for its continuance; the latter enslaved men's minds as it depended upon the fear of spiritual punishment. Neither, he was convinced, could be eliminated by less than wholehearted commitment to the ultimate cause of human liberation; and, whereas Ingersoll was willing to compromise objective truth as he saw it in the courtroom or on the political stump, he was never willing to do so in his war with orthodox theology or in his pronouncements of his faith in man.

Ingersoll's convictions had their inception in two areas: in his personal experience with and knowledge of the religion of John Calvin, one of the most demeaning theological structures in the history of Western thought, and in his introduction to the rationalism of the eighteenth century, one of the most ennobling philosophical structures of human history. When the two collided, as they had more than a century before in the thinking of Benjamin Franklin, the resulting conflict was resolved by a triumph of reason that was permanent and complete—so complete in Ingersoll's case that his major criticism of the eighteenth-century Enlightenment was that it stopped short of completely routing the forces of superstitious irrationality.

Ingersoll's convictions were as completely based on faith as the theology that he criticized; but his faith was in science, the product of men's "Reason, Observation, and Experience—the Holy Trinity of Science"—rather than upon the personalized deity of the orthodox. He was firmly convinced that his trinity was the only means whereby man could and would find ultimate salvation, a salvation of perfection in this world rather than in the next. Reason, he insisted, teaches men that this world is the only reality they can know, and they must stand or fall on this earth rather than in a speculative hereafter.

The freely inquiring mind, the mind characterized by rational inquiry, was the only means whereby man could find salvation, according to Ingersoll; and his revelation was science. Man, he insisted, could find truth only by applying his mind to the tangible universe and then correlating the results. Ingersoll found much support and justification for his faith in the accomplishments and discoveries of science since Isaac Newton had provided the basic tool and had pointed the way. Ingersoll, neither a scientist nor a philosopher, was well aware of the increasing domain of science and of the decreasing realm of the supernatural; and to him the evidence was conclusive as it culminated, in his time, in the pronouncements of Charles Darwin. The *Origin of Species* was to Ingersoll merely the culminating evidence of a rational science that had long before eliminated the supernatural as an acceptable explanation of the origin of the universe.

But Ingersoll's faith in science was not characterized by a belief in a rigidly determined naturalistic universe. Unlike many of his colleagues, he believed that man in his natural state was a free being, controlling and expanding his own destiny; and he was equally convinced that man would some day rid himself of superstitions and attain that natural state. His rationalism, then, was coexistent with his humanism, his faith in man; and he would not accept one without the other.

If his rationalism was a product, intensified, of the eighteenth century, his humanism, equally intensified, was of the nineteenth, of the philosophical idealism and the democratic faith that dominated the America of his youth. Purged of any overtones of the supernatural by his relentless reason, his humanism was based nevertheless upon Emerson's dictum that man must know himself, upon Thoreau's assertion that he must reform himself, and upon Jackson's conviction that the free man is intuitively wise. A "frontier democrat" in both senses of the term, Ingersoll never lost his faith in man and in man's destiny, even in the heat of his political defense of the sound dollar and the high tariff, because he saw nothing mutually exclusive in conservative economics, religious iconoclasm, and democratic humanism. To him, they were the three tangible roots of an intangible but real human freedom.

But Ingersoll did not systematize his thoughts, convictions, and evidence—nor did he have any intention of doing so. From the beginning of his devotion to what Thomas Henry Huxley had termed "agnosticism" and which Ingersoll had fused with humanism, he saw his role much as his father had earlier seen his: he was the preacher of agnostic humanism just as John Ingersoll had been the preacher of God's word as interpreted by John Calvin, and there was from the beginning much of the father in the son.

Without question Ingersoll patterned what he knew of the formalities of public speaking upon what he had learned from his father, and his lectures are in the tradition of the great religious oratory of the nineteenth cenutry. In propagating his doctrine, he almost invariably used two approaches: one was the negative, in which he proposed to shock his audience into disbelief much as religious forebears attempted to shock theirs into the opposite; the second was the positive, in which he constructed the image of the perfection attainable by believers in the new faith. In both approaches, often appearing consecutively in the same lecture, Ingersoll combined the relentlessness of logic and the emotional appeal of faith; he cemented them with a strong infusion of showmanship; and he presented them with his intensely dramatic instinct for appearance, language, analogy, sound, and rhythm. The result was invariably powerful.

I *"The Gods"*

Although Ingersoll's convictions on matters of religion, science, God, and man were largely fixed by the time he entered the army in 1861—he gave his first anti-theological lecture, "Progress," in Pekin, Illinois, in 1860—and his major impact as a nationally known agnostic lecturer was made in the years following his nomination of "Plumed Knight" Blaine in 1876, he began his major assault of the fortress of theology with the writing and presentation of "The Gods" in 1872. "Progress" had paved the way; but its tone was reticent, its major enemy was physical rather than intellectual slavery, and its emphasis was upon a faith in change wrought through natural intellectual evolution rather than through a headlong assault and proselytizing missionary work. In "Progress," Ingersoll's faith was in the fact of change for the better. In "The Gods," he was determined to help bring it about,

It is evident that Ingersoll had done carefully and well his preparatory research for "The Gods"; not only are his scholarly references, theological summaries, and references to comparative religious phenomena well founded; they are also accurate. None of Ingersoll's religious critics has been able to find more than minor errors of fact in his evidence. It is, of course, the interpretations of those facts which Ingersoll's critics dispute; and, as he wrote "The Gods," he was well aware of the necessity for irrefutable scholarship, as he wrote to his brother, Ebon Clark. Interestingly enough, at the time, as the letter indicates, he had some doubts about the desirability of publishing the essay, a quandary that was never again to present itself:

I am not writing my lecture or book on "The Gods." I have concluded to take your advice and expand what I intended for a preface into a small work or lecture.

As soon as I get it written I will send it to you and get your idea as to the propriety of its publication.

The subject is really a vast one, and requires a great deal more learning than I have.

I wish I could have access to the Library in Washington for a few days. It will, however, be utterly impossible for me to go to Washington this winter. . . .[11]

Nevertheless, "The Gods" as written and delivered shows Ingersoll's audacity rather than reticence. His initial assault was on the origin and nature of the anthropomorphic god, the god personalized by the attachment to him of human traits, however multiplied or magnified. He began the study with a parody of Alexander Pope, insisting that "An honest God is the noblest work of Man," thus pointing out the direction of his thrust with dramatic precision.

The first part of the essay is devoted to delineating and decrying, while ostensibly presenting in objective outline, man's fear of, and respect for, the unknown and the unknowable. But the apparent objectivity disappears quickly as Ingersoll applies the eighteenth-century, rapierlike questions of rational analysis to his evidence. But, unlike the rationalists of the Enlightenment, he respects no self-evident and hence unquestioned and unquestionable truths; and he reinforces his questions with a terminology and an emphasis designed to reduce the supernatural to ridiculousness by any rational terms. The coup de grace is delivered by an equally pointed and rapid wit:

Each nation has created a god, and the god has always resembled his creators. He hated and loved what they hated and loved, and he was invariably found on the side of those in power. Each god was intensely patriotic, and detested all nations but his own. All these gods demanded praise, flattery, and worship. Most of them were pleased with sacrifice, and the smell of innocent blood has ever been considered a divine perfume. All these gods have insisted upon having a vast number of priests, and and the priests have always insisted upon being supported by the people. . . . (I, 7)

After the unqualified definitiveness of his opening pronouncement, he then delivers a witty blow that is devastating in its implications:

Most of these gods were revengeful, savage, lustful, and ignorant. As they generally depended upon their priests for information, their ignorance can hardly excite our astonishment.

These gods did not even know the shape of the worlds they had created, but supposed them to be flat. Some thought the day could be lengthened by stopping the sun, that the blowing of horns could throw down the walls of a city, and all knew so little of the real nature of the people they had created, that they commanded the people to love them. Some were so ignorant as to suppose that man could believe just as he might desire, or as they might command, and that to be governed by observation, reason, and experience was a most foul and damning sin. None of these gods could give a true account of the creation of this little earth. All were woefully deficient in geology and astronomy. As a rule, they were most miserable legislators, and as executives, they were far inferior to the average of American presidents. (I, 8–9)

Particularly remarkable in Ingersoll's performance thus far is the fact that he has discussed not God but gods, the pluralistic array of primitive deities with which human history and prehistory are replete, and he presumably has not ventured from the path of orthodox abhorrence of paganism. But Ingersoll, like Emerson in *Nature,* is actually loading the dice; and he makes clear, by such unmistakable biblical references as those to Joshua and Jericho, that the Old Testament God of the Jews, the forerunner of the God of Christianity, is no exception. Thus, in his apparent references to pagan gods, demonstrating their brutality and inhumanity, as well as their basic dishonesty, he prepares the way for identical charges against the Judeo–Christian God:

One of these gods, and one who demands our love, our admiration, and our worship, and one who is worshiped, if mere heartless ceremony is worship, gave to his chosen people for their guidance, the following laws of war: "When thou comest nigh unto a city to fight against it, *then proclaim peace unto it.* And it shall be if it make thee answer of peace, and open unto thee, then it shall be that all the people that is found therein shall be tributaries unto thee, and they shall serve thee. And if it will make no peace with thee, but will make war against thee, then thou shalt besiege it. And when the Lord thy God hath delivered it into thy hands, thou shalt smite every male thereof with the edge of the sword. . . . But of the cities of these people which the Lord thy God doth give thee for an inheritance, *thou shalt save nothing alive that breatheth.*" (I, 12–13)

To Ingersoll there is only one possible rational deduction; such behavior is certainly not worthy of reverence, nor can such a being deserve worship: "And we are called upon to worship such a God; to get upon our knees and tell him that he is good, that he is merciful, that he is just, that he is love . . . ." (I, 13–14). Turning then immediately to the offensive, he defiantly proclaimed: "Let the people hate, let the god threaten—we will educate them, and we will despise and defy him" (I, 14).

To Ingersoll the Bible is not the record of man's evolutionary and progressive concept of the nature of God as he changes from a vicious, petty tribal God in man's view, thereby reflecting man's nature, to a just, humane, and loving God, reflecting a more civilized man, as Andrew Dickinson White insisted; to Ingersoll the God of the Bible is one, the Jehovah of the Israelites and the wrathful God of the Calvinists; and as such, if He exists, He is unworthy not only of worship but of man's notice.

But Ingersoll's implications are clear; the only reality of such a God lies in the ignorance and supersitition of the men who created Him in their own image, and he sees that man is slowly but surely beginning to deny Him existence:

The people are beginning to think, to reason and to investigate. Slowly, painfully, but surely, the gods are being driven from the earth. Only upon rare occasions are they, even by the most religious, supposed to interfere in the affairs of men. . . . As a general thing, the gods have stopped drowning children, except as a punishment for violating the Sabbath. They still pay some attention to the affairs of kings, men of genius and persons of great wealth; but ordinary people are left to shirk for themselves as best they may. In wars between great nations, the gods still interfere; but in prize fights, the best man with an honest referee, is almost sure to win. (I, 40–41)

With his final barb, Ingersoll turns away from what is actually an artfully broad and carefully shocking assault on orthodoxy to an approach less rhetorical, less dramatic, but more valid: the examination, by reason but without theatrics or shock therapy, of the question of God's existence. First, he attacks the concept of creation, the essence of the theological explanation of God's nature, power, and role in the universe. The implications to Ingersoll are clear: the theological theory of Creation, revealed in Genesis, has neither evidence nor logic to support it; scientific explanations, insisting that matter and force can be neither created nor destroyed, have both. The theological theory of the First Cause, he insists, demands a halt in the process of cause and effect; and it has no evidence other than the miraculous, in itself a logical impossibility contrary to reason and experience.

Again, to Ingersoll the implications are clear: perhaps one does not know what the ultimate truth is, but one's reason tells one what it is not; and he concludes by constructing upon the foundations of that which he has destroyed. In passing, he denies the possibility of a creative or theistic evolution like that accepted by liberal theologians such as Henry Ward Beecher; such, he insists, is both absurd and unnecessary. Ingersoll concludes with a vision of the future in which rational man, rather than a petty, tyrannical God, has captured the loyalty and fealty of men:

> We are laying the foundations of the grand temple of the future—not the temple of all the gods, but of all the people—wherein, with appropriate rites, will be celebrated the religion of Humanity. We are doing what little we can to hasten the coming of the day when society shall cease producing millionaires and mendicants—gorged indolence and famished industry—truth in rags and superstition robed and crowned. We are looking for the time when the useful shall be the honorable; and when Reason, throned upon the world's brain, shall be the King of Kings, and God of Gods. (I, 89—90)

"The Gods" epitomizes Ingersoll's rationalistic assault on religious orthodoxy, which he equated with superstition, and also his positive substitution for that orthodoxy as they remained for the rest of his life. In "The Gods," as in almost all of his lectures on religion and rationalism, he employed many of the same techniques that he had employed in his courtroom addresses and his political speeches. In each, he had a cause, whether a client, a candidate, a party, or a belief; and, in each, he combined attack and defense, destructive if often overstated criticism with positive, if equally often overstated, suggestion and assertion. The results in each case were generally effective, if controversial; and the means whereby those ends were achieved were subordinated to them.

The essay illustrates at the same time the techniques that Ingersoll employed. He was not, nor would he be, a declaimer in the classic oratorical tradition; rather, he was, in the American pulpit and stump tradition, forceful and forthright, maintaining a headlong pace from beginning to end. At the same time, his sentence structure and word choices were designed to expedite that pace. Not a flowery orator in either structure, metaphor, or vocabulary, as many of his contemporaries were, Ingersoll chose a basic sentence pattern that was short, active, and forceful; his vocabulary was almost invariably blunt, vivid, and concrete, the words primarily of Anglo-Saxon rather than Latin origin. Combined with this style were wit and imagery out of and close to the people who made up his audiences—the shopkeepers, printers, clerks, and students as well as farmers and others. He did not address himself to the intellectuals but to the people, and his total style was natively and democratically American as a result. The combination produced a dynamic liveliness that reached, captured, and retained his audience to the end. This air of the immediacy of life not only accounted for much of his popularity but also made him appear to stand personally in symbolic opposition to ideas that were lifeless and deadly.

From the point of view of Ingersoll's career, "The Gods" was particularly significant. The strength of his attack, the forthrightness of his position, and the uncompromising relentlessness and ferociousness of his examination combined to make it sensational and to make him America's most famous religious critic almost immediately. Hostility directed by the orthodox clergy toward Darwin, Huxley, and others of the new scientific skepticism was largely redirected toward Ingersoll; and he became the symbol of heresy, of sin, and of danger. His reluctance to make "The Gods" public was perhaps justified, but he would not and could not retreat once he began.

Among the clerical voices raised in condemnation of "The Gods" and of Ingersoll personally, one clergyman, the most famous and respected of his day both as a preacher and as a man, spoke in his defense: Henry Ward Beecher, who was later to share political platforms and condemnation with Ingersoll and ultimately to become his friend. In his publication, *The Christian Union,* for May 15, 1872, just after the publication of "The Gods," Beecher wrote:

Some good people of Central Illinois are much exercised by one of the utterances of a lawyer, Colonel Robert G. Ingersoll, who has the temerity to pervert the words of (not *the*) Pope, and says: "An honest God is the noblest work of man." It strikes us as a very ingenious parody, and a very sensible remark. Every man constructs his God out of the materials that are furnished him. We are ready to see the physical and mental deformity of the gods the heathen make; are there not some built up out of soulless formularies and logical inferences that are scarcely less repulsive? The *least* we can ask of theology would seem to be an "honest God"; but, if we take theology to include all that is good and pure, just and true, we may accept the epigram of the Free-thinker, and say that to give us such an ideal of our Creator and our Redeemer would be its "noblest work." [2]

For Beecher, whose own God bore little resemblance to that of his father, the Reverend Lyman Beecher, or to that of the Reverend John Ingersoll, and whose God was also to undergo additional change as the guiding spirit behind theistic evolution, recognition of a vigorously but validly questioning mind was easy; but for his colleagues in the clergy it was almost entirely impossible. The ensuing condemnation, continuing in some circles almost unabatedly to the present, indicated clearly what the clerical attitude toward Ingersoll was to be. But with Ingersoll's reputation as an agnostic orator secure, and with his "call" finally found, Ingersoll, perhaps captured by the same heady sensation as he was to find in the political campaign of 1876, took to his own pulpit.

II *"Individuality"*

Ingersoll followed "The Gods" with "Individuality," written in 1873, in which he sought to identify and describe the great human good that would result from man's rejection of superstition in the form of orthodox religion. Whereas in "The Gods," Ingersoll's point of attack was clear from the beginning and remained in focus until the end, Ingersoll in "Individuality" insisted that the real enemy of individuality was not merely orthodox theology but institutions and customs of many kinds. They were enemies wherever they combined to inhibit or thwart man's search for his fullest, most free development. However, the churches of Calvin and of Rome— of "Thou shalt nots" and of dogmatic demands on credibility—were to him the most inhibiting and frustrating of institutions; and their customs were the most damning.

Nevertheless, in spite of its theological evidence and sharp rending of theological cloth into shreds, "Individuality" is more restrained and its impact less shocking than "The Gods." But that comparison is only relative, as Ingersoll began almost immediately to question some of the most widely accepted and consequently most powerfully inhibiting of man's beliefs:

On every hand are the enemies of individuality and mental freedom. Custom meets us at the cradle and leaves us only at the tomb. Our first questions are answered by ignorance, and our last by superstition. We are pushed and dragged by countless hands along the beaten track, and our entire training can be summed up in the word—suppression.

... We are allowed to investigate all subjects in which we feel no particular interest, and to express the opinions of the majority with the utmost freedom. We are taught that liberty of speech should never be carried to the extent of contradicting the dead witnesses of a popular superstition. Society offers continual rewards for self-betrayal, and they are nearly all earned and claimed, and some are paid. ... (I, 169–70)

Here Ingersoll sounds more like a more forceful Emerson proclaiming his gospel of self-reliance or a more waspish Thoreau surveying the quiet desperation of Concord, and there are many parallels between the pleas of Transcendentalism and of Ingersoll's rationalism, not only in their demands for human liberty, but also in their faith in man's ability to make proper use of that freedom once it has been attained. But the analogy is dangerously misleading beyond this point, in spite of a mutual distrust of man's institutions. Emerson's goal for man is union with God; Ingersoll's is finding pride and dignity in his manhood. But the parallels in means continue, as Ingersoll preaches an ideal for a commonplace rather than an esoteric "American Scholar":

The trouble with most people is, they bow to what is called authority; they have a certain reverence for the old because it is old. They think a man is better for being dead, especially if he has been dead a long time. They think the fathers of their nation were the greatest and best of all mankind. All these things they implicitly believe because it is popular and patriotic, and because they were told so when they were very small, and remember distinctly of hearing mother read it out of a book. It is hard to overestimate the influence of early training in the direction of superstition. You first teach children that a book is true—that it was written by God himself—that to question its truth is a sin, that to deny it is a crime, and that should they die without believing that book they will be forever damned without benefit of clergy. The consequence is, long before they read that book their minds are wholly unfitted to investigate its claims. They accept it as a matter of course. ... (I, 171–72)

From his attack upon the pressures that demand conformity and orthodoxy in thinking and behavior, Ingersoll turned to his positive statement of faith, a faith that has echoes of Emerson's "Self-Reliance" and of Thoreau's distant but separate drummer. But again he attacked and permitted his statement to remain on the level of assertion without, as Emerson attempted to do, probing the ends and meaning of that individualism:

> In my judgement, every human being should take a road of his own. Every mind should be true to itself—should think, investigate and conclude for itself. This is a duty alike incumbent upon pauper and prince. Every soul should repel dictation and tyranny, no matter from what source they come—from earth or heaven, from men to gods. Besides, every traveler upon this vast plain should give to every other traveler his best idea as to the road that should be taken. Each is entitled to the honest opinion of all. And there is but one way to get an honest opinion upon any subject whatever. The person giving the opinion must be free from fear. The merchant must not fear to lose his custom, the doctor his practice, nor the preacher his pulpit. There can be no advance without liberty. Suppression of honest inquiry is retrogression, and must end in intellectual night. The tendency of orthodox religion today is toward mental slavery and barbarism. . . . Every pulpit is a pillory, in which stands a hired culprit, defending the justice of his own imprisonment. (I, 179—80)

In concluding his plea for individualism, Ingersoll contrasted the lot of the free man with that of the slave to orthodoxy. His conclusion is reminiscent of his closing remarks in the courtroom and on the political stump as he re-created the contrast between the two fates in an emotional appeal:

> It is the duty of each and every one to maintain his individuality. "This above all, to thine own-self be true, and it must follow as the night the day, thou canst not then be false to any man." It is a magnificent thing to be the sole proprietor of yourself. . . . It is humiliating to know that your ideas are all borrowed; that you are indebted to your memory for your principles; that your religion is simply one of your habits, and that you would have convictions if they were only contagious . . . that you reap what the great and brave have sown, and that you can benefit the world only by leaving it. (I, 204—05)

"Individuality" is not one of Ingersoll's greatest orations; in comparison to "The Gods," "Some Mistakes of Moses," "Why I Am An

Agnostic," and others of the more militant and powerful orations, it remains on the level of generality; and the powerful rhetorical flourishes of the others are absent. But it remained one of Ingersoll's most popular as well as least controversial lectures, and its close relationship to the mainstream of liberal thinking in nineteenth-century America has given it permanence. Perhaps of most importance, however, is the fact that it remains Ingersoll's clearest demand for the freedom of inquiry that he sought, and it also occupies a central role among those declarations of intellectual independence which played such a prominent role in the development of a pluralistic, intellectually free atmosphere for the growth of intellectual America.

III   *"Heretics and Heresies"*

In "Heretics and Heresies," written in 1874, Ingersoll returned to a thesis that he had tentatively explored in "Progress," his first important public address, and that gave him much personal delight as well as self-confidence throughout his life. Actually an extension of "Individualism" as it was written, it was based upon Ingersoll's conviction that any man who pursues individualism, integrity, or honesty is, by the definition of the orthodox, a heretic; and his thoughts or works, by virtue of the fact that they are his, are heresy. Just as he took pleasure in the term "infidel" and used it in reference to himself, he made, in this essay, the term "heretic" a name to be worn with pride.

Again, as in "The Gods," he makes his attack barbed and detailed as he examines the crimes of specific religious denominations. He gives special attention to the Bible as a source of evil and to John Calvin as one who personified it in the name of good. In indicting the former, he raises the question of its power rhetorically:

The Bible was the real persecutor. The Bible burned heretics, built dungeons, founded the Inquisition, and trampled upon the liberties of men.

How long, O how long will mankind worship a book? How long will they grovel in the dust before the ignorant legends of the barbaric past? How long, O how long will they pursue phantoms in a darkness deeper than death? (I, 222)

For John Calvin, however, no such rhetoric was necessary; a simple recital of the facts with a minimum of embellishment or editorial comment was sufficient to make Ingersoll's point:

Unfortunately for the world, about the beginning of the sixteenth century, a man by the name of Gerard Chauvin was married to Jeanne Lefranc, and still more unfortunately for the world, the fruit of this marriage was a son, called John Chauvin, who afterwards became famous as John Calvin the founder of the Presbyterian Church.

This man forged five fetters for the brain. These fetters he called points. That is to say, predestination, particular redemption, total depravity, irresistible grace, and the perseverance of the saints. About the neck of each follower he put a collar bristling with these five points. The presence of all these points is still the test of orthodoxy in the church he founded. . . . Liberty was banished from Geneva, and nothing but Presbyterianism was left. . . .

The best thing, however, about the Presbyterians of Geneva was, that they denied the power of the Pope, and the best thing about the Pope, was that he was not a Presbyterian. . . . (I, 222–27)

Particularly pointed is Ingersoll's examination of the charges, point by point, leveled against an Illinois minister accused of heresy by his fellow Presbyterians. In each of the twelve charges, most of them resulting from doubts about the eternal truth inherent in the five points, Ingersoll points out absurdities, inconsistencies, and evidences of the brutality inherent in all religious inquisitions. But, as in the other attacks on the orthodoxy, Ingersoll ended by attempting to give his audience a vision of something greater in exchange for discarding its faith:

How long, O how long, will man listen to the threats of God, and shut his eyes to the splendid possibilities of Nature? How long, O how long will man remain the cringing slave of a false and cruel creed?

By this time the whole world should know that the real Bible has not yet been written, but is being written, and that it will never be finished until the race begins its downward march, or ceases to exist?

. . . This book appeals to all the surroundings of man. Each thing that exists testifies of its perfection. The earth, with its heart of fire and crowns of snow; with its forests and plains, its rocks and seas; with its every wave and cloud; with its every leaf and bud and flower, confirms its every word, and the solemn stars shining in the infinite abysses, are the eternal witnesses of its truth. (I, 252–53)

IV *"Ghosts"*

In 1877, Ingersoll wrote both "Ghosts" and "The Liberty of Man, Woman, and Child," each in its own way an important work in the

Ingersoll canon. The former, an attack on the forces of orthodoxy, is so strong that it engendered bitter responses from the clergy and resulted in his strong response, "My Reviewers Reviewed." Like the others, "Ghosts" attacked orthodoxy as the remnant of ghosts that have, since the beginning of time, haunted men ridden by ignorance and fear. But, as Ingersoll points out, man's intellectual advances have limited both the number and domain of those ghosts. Nevertheless, the record of crimes inspired by those ghosts and by their believers and followers is impressive and frightening; for evidence, Ingersoll re-creates the history of the prosecution of witches, and the implications concerning the tradition out of which religious orthodoxy has come are clear, damning, and direct.

Ingersoll's scholarship, most of it utilized dispassionately, is impressive if highly selective; and in totality it leaves little for his opponents to emphasize as proof of virtue. Wisely, Ingersoll lets the facts speak for themselves, as in this quotation from one of the most revered legal commentators in the history of English and American legal codes and jurisprudence:

> Sir William Blackstone, in his Commentaries on the Laws of England, says: "To deny the possibility, nay, actual existence of witchcraft and sorcery, is at once flatly to contradict the word of God in various passages both of the Old and New Testament; and the thing itself is a truth to which every nation in the world hath in its turn borne testimony, either by examples seemingly well attested, or by prohibitory laws, which at least suppose the possibility of a commerce with evil spirits." (I, 279)

This passage and others like it are evidence to Ingersoll of the power exerted by ghosts over men's minds, a power that can only be overcome by progress; and, as he calls the role of contributors and contributions to the progress of man, he makes it clear that the freely inquiring mind can and will lay the remaining ghosts as easily and surely as they have witchcraft:

> Every fact has pushed a superstition from the brain and a ghost from the clouds. Every mechanic art is an educator. Every loom, every reaper and mower, every steamboat, every locomotive, every engine, every press, every telegraph, is a missionary of Science and an apostle of Progress. Every mill, every furnace, every building with its wheels and levers, in which something is made for the convenience, for the use, and for the comfort and elevation of man, is a church, and every schoolhouse is a temple. . . . (I, 312–13)

From this testimonial eulogy of mechanical progress as a means of freeing man not only physically but intellectually and morally, Ingersoll calls the roll of those who have contributed to laying the ghosts of the past, from Columbus and Galileo to Robert Fulton and Samuel F. B. Morse, each of whom has increased the realm of man's knowledge and power and decreased the dominion of the ghosts. "We are," he says, "beginning to learn that to exchange a mistake for the truth—a superstition for a fact—to ascertain the real—is to progress" (I, 315).

Ingersoll concludes with his vision of the future, one which incorporates faith in man and in progress much as a younger, less restrained Emerson might have described it. But again Ingersoll stops short of Emerson's vision of the ultimate; his faith is firmly rooted in man and the earth:

. . . Let the ghosts go—we will worship them no more. Man is greater than these phantoms. Humanity is grander than all the creeds, than all the books. Humanity is the great sea, and these creeds, and books, and religions, are but the waves of a day. Humanity is the sky, and these religions and dogmas and theories are but the mists and clouds changing continually, destined finally to melt away.

That which is founded upon slavery, and fear, and ignorance, cannot endure. In the religion of the future, there will be men and women and children, all the aspirations of the soul, and all the tender humanities of the heart.

Let the ghosts go. We will worship them no more. Let them cover their eyeless sockets with their fleshless hands and fade forever from the imaginations of men. (I, 326)

V *"The Liberty of Man, Woman, and Child"*

"Ghosts" was in essence prefatory to "The Libery of Man, Woman, and Child," written in the same year and designed to be a major statement on the nature of the intellectual freedom that Ingersoll sought. Like "The Gods" and the later "Why I Am An Agnostic," it was intended to be and was a major statement of position, and it lies midway between the two in significance and emphasis. The first was a major assault on the forces of orthodox religion; the second, a major positive statement expressing faith in man and in liberty; and the last, a documentary account of his own intellectual emancipation. In "The Liberty of Man, Woman, and Child," he began to articulate the humanistic principles which, rooted in human intellectual liberty and growing to incorporate all human good and happiness, were to become in the future increasingly prominent in his thinking and speaking as well as in his own personal life. The lecture remains his major statement on the subject and a major defense of human freedom.

Ingersoll deliberately divided the topic into three areas of emphasis, recognizing as he did the intensity with which not one standard but many standards are enforced on men; and two standards especially, those applied to women and to children, were of great concern to him. The first part is a general statement on the history and significance of human liberty; the second is devoted to a detailed examination of the reality and the ideal as applied to women; and the third defines both as they apply to children. His conclusion, as before, is an appeal for and a tribute to progress. In each, pithy, barbed accusations are evident, but they are minor in the light of the statements of principle and of belief that Ingersoll emphasizes.

Ingersoll's opening statement is neither shocking, condemnatory, nor challenging, as it was in *"The Gods."* Instead, it is a reasoned, provocative statement that is at once a logical proposition and a statement of belief, simply phrased: "Liberty sustains the same Relationship to Mind that Space does to Matter." Ingersoll maintains his focus upon that statement as he examines the state and pleads the cause of liberty.

To him, slavery and freedom are effects, he asserts at the beginning: slavery is the effect of ignorance; liberty, of intelligence. He looks at these relationships carefully, by examining first the effects of ignorance as it attempts to regulate thought and force conformity, and then the slowly accelerating force of growing knowledge as it creates growing freedom. As he examines the forces of ignorance, his descriptions are graphic as he portrays the use of the thumbscrew, the collar of torture, the scavenger's daughter, and finally the rack; in each case, the instrument of torture was applied by ignorant forces to enforce conformity and faith and to produce recantations. Ingersoll's reaction to these visions is as vivid and forceful as the description of the instruments:

Sometimes, when I read and think about these frightful things it seems to me that I have suffered all these horrors myself. . . . And when I so feel, I swear that while I live I will do what little I can to preserve and to augment the liberties of man, woman, and child.

It is a question of justice, of mercy, of honesty, of intellectual development. If there is a man in the world who is not willing to give to every human being every right he claims for himself, he is just so much nearer a barbarian than I am. It is a question of honesty. The man who is not willing to give to every other the same intellectual rights he claims for himself, is dishonest, selfish, and brutal.

It is a question of intellectual development. Whoever holds another man responsible for his honest thought, has a deformed and distorted brain. . . . (I, 337–39)

But Ingersoll compares man's ingenious development and use of instruments of torture with his scientific development as shown in the progress of ships from dugouts to steamships, of musical instruments, of paintings and sculpture, and finally, in the development of man himself, as shown in the skulls that trace his evolution. The suggestion for the future is clear: "The first and lowest skull in this row was the den in which crawled the base and meaner instincts of mankind, and the last was a temple in which dwelt joy, liberty, and love" (I, 342).

With the human potential for progress and for ultimate perfection so evident, Ingersoll examines the lot of woman, particularly of woman in relationship to man; and he produces at once a tribute to the love of women and a denunciation of those who abuse it. But he does not come to grips with the liberty of woman as the feminists of the time insisted that it must be; instead, he eulogizes the home based upon love and respect as the source of liberty for the family as a unit. "I believe in the fireside," he says. "I believe in the democracy of home. I believe in the republicanism of the family. I believe in liberty, equality, and love." Unfortunately, however, Ingersoll implies too clearly that the equality of woman and man can only be given and guaranteed by man—a position no feminist could accept.

Ingersoll's position on children—perhaps stemming from his own memories of an authoritarian home which contrasted with the permissive atmosphere in which he and his wife reared their two daughters—is a mixture of freedom and love, of homely advice and vivid memory. In taking this position, he parallels his comments on the liberty of women; for one finds no recognition of the children in factories or on the farms, for whom life was a harsh struggle for survival. To Ingersoll, unfortunately, it seems that the child's world is in either a permissive or an authortarian middle-class home. He concludes, with more sentimental rhetoric than logic, that "Men are oaks, women are vines, children are flowers," and with another rhetorical address to a liberty that remains an abstraction: "Oh Liberty, float not forever in the far horizon—remain not forever in the dream of the enthusiast, the philanthropist and poet, but come and make thy home among the children of men. . . (I, 398).

It is unfortunate that this lecture, in which Ingersoll planned to make a major statement on the nature of the need for, and the reality of liberty, did not do what he intended. Instead of a definitive statement examining liberty in his time, particularly in relationship to women and children, Ingersoll takes refuge in sentimentality and unreality; and the result is a pathetically superficial and pale imitation of his major efforts at dispute and definition. Undoubtedly one of his most deeply felt orations, it is also one of his weakest in its clear indication of the shallowness of his thinking about the reality of the lack of liberty in the nineteenth century.

This shortcoming points out one of Ingersoll's basic weaknesses in stating his beliefs and convictions on matters that go beyond purely religious matters. Almost invariably he shows a limited grasp of the problem, and he consequently promises much more than it is possible for him to deliver to his listeners or readers. Nowhere is this more evident than in his treatment of contemporary social problems such as those concerning the liberty of what he sweepingly entitles "Man, Woman, and Child." Perhaps the result of a conflict between his conservative economic convictions and his innate sympathy for human beings, but more probably a result of his economic ignorance and social shortsightedness and consequently an inability rather than an unwillingness to perceive the harsh economic reality behind the illusion of freedom in the new industrial system, Ingersoll's social criticism is invariably narrow and sentimental, focusing upon shortcomings in middle-class relations rather than upon those between classes. Ingersoll was a kind man as well as one innately sympathetic to the underdog; consequently, ignorance rather than viciousness seems the logical explanation.

VI   *"What Must We Do to be Saved?"*

However, when Ingersoll returned to his examination of the dogmatic assertions of various Christian sects in "What Must We Do to be Saved?," published in 1880, he was on much more solid ground. Again, he based his arguments on careful research rather than on generality; and he ranged widely in showing the major inconsistencies not only among the sects but in the Gospels of the New Testament upon which those sects base their convictions. His major accusation against the churches is that they are dishonest, either through ignorance or deliberately; consequently, none can be believed. In his introduction he questions the concept of salvation; it is not, he insists, salvation from poverty, crime, or tyranny but from the wrath of man's Creator who must ultimately be held responsible for the actions and shortcomings of his product. At the heart of the concept, then, he insists, there is either illogicality or viciousness.

In his comparison of the gospels of the four evangelists, he discovers a curious inconsistency that reveals dogmatic assertions to be untrue. In the first three gospels he finds a doctrine of love and forgiveness; the conclusion, he then insists, is unescapable:

Read Matthew, Mark, and Luke, and then read John, and you will agree with me that the three first gospels teach that if we are kind and forgiving to our follows, God will be kind and forgiving to us. In John we are told that another man can be good for us, or bad for us, and that the only way to get to heaven is to believe something that we know is not so.

All these passages about believing in Christ, drinking his blood and eating his flesh, are afterthoughts. They were written by the theologians, and in a few years they will be considered unworthy of the lips of Christ. (I, 489–90)

Ingersoll then examines the specific requirements of the Roman Catholics, the Episcopalians, the Methodists, his favorite Presbyterians, and the Evangelical Alliance in which a number of fundamentalist sects joined in a common creed. In each case, his conclusions are the same: the requirements are monstrous and unbelievable; they are vicious and illogical; they have nothing in common either with the virtues of love and mercy preached by Christ or with the dogmas of one another.

In his final section, Ingersoll proposes a substitution of the values of humanism for the dogmas of the churches. Essentially a forceful resume of his own convictions and values, the section is again Ingersoll at his most skillful and eloquent as he combines force, rapid movement, and sentiment to produce his final plea. In many way, it summarizes the values by which he lived:

. . . I propose good fellowship—good friends all around. . . .

. . . I believe in the gospel of Cheerfulness, the gospel of Good Nature, the gospel of Good Health. . . .

. . . I believe in the gospel of Good Living. . . . of good clothes . . . of good houses . . . of water and soap . . . of intelligence. . . . of education . . . of justice, that we must reap what we sow. . . .

And I believe, too, in the gospel of Liberty . . . the gospel of Intelligence. . . . Humanity—that word embraces all there is.

So I believe in this great gospel of Humanity. . . . (I, 517–22)

His final lines, devoid of denunciation, are among the most forceful and most positive that Ingersoll ever delivered. In various forms he repeated them in numerous future similar statements:

I have made up my mind that if there is a God, he will be merciful to the merciful.

Upon that rock I stand.—

That he will not torture the forgiving.—

Upon that rock I stand.—

That every man shall be true to himself, and that there is no world, no star, in which honesty is a crime.

Upon that rock I stand.

The honest man, the good man, the happy child, having nothing to fear, either in this world or the world to come.

Upon that rock I stand. (I, 325)

VII   *"Some Mistakes of Moses"*

Paired with Ingersoll's rational and humanistic assault upon the foundations of Christian faith and dogma is "Some Mistakes of Moses," an attack upon the foundations of the Old Testament in the Pentateuch. Ingersoll's attack is focused upon the orthodox assertion that the Bible is the inspired word of God, and he supports his assault with his customary evidence against the nature of God as Christians see him. Both examinations are detailed: the first is based upon contrary scientific evidence, much of it accepted by modern contemporary Christians; the other is founded upon his own contrary humanistic convictions. Again, for Ingersoll the conclusions are inevitable; if the Bible is the inspired word of God, it must be entirely so; and the evidence of astronomy, geology, botany, zoology, and other sciences— all of them used by Ingersoll in his examination—is false; or conversely, none of it is true. The Christian cannot pick and choose what he believes to be inspired and what not, meanwhile hiding behind the general assertion that it is the inspired word of God. "It was," he insists, "produced by ignorance, and has been believed and defended by its author" (II, 242).

Even more determined is Ingersoll's attack upon those who insist that, although biblical science may be uninspired, its morality is certainly dictated by God. At that point, Ingersoll examines its morality: its acceptance of slavery; of polygamy; of aggressive, selfish, and unjust war; and of religious, social, and cultural prejudice and persecution. His conclusion is simple but logical, and in it he approximates the view of Andrew Dickinson White that, in each phase, the Bible is a record of the values and conditions of its time: "Is it not far better and wiser to say that the Pentateuch, while containing some good laws, some truths, some wise and useful things is, after all, deformed and blackened by the savagery of its time? Is it not far better and wiser to take the good and throw the bad away? " (II, 265).

But Ingersoll was not willing to let his arguments rest at this point; and, insisting that men "admit what they know to be true," he catalogues the long list of errors, of shortcomings, of lapses in what man now accepts as moral behavior and concludes with a demand that "every free, brave, and enlightened man should publicly declare that all the ignorant, infamous, heartless, hideous things recorded in the 'inspired' Pentateuch are not the words of God, but simply 'Some Mistakes of Moses' " (II, 270).

Were it not for his lapses into polemic and into the antagonistic rhetoric of his conclusions, Ingersoll might have written, in "Some Mistakes of Moses, " an important, brief critical analysis of the first five books of the Bible. But, unfortunately, the orator, the baiter, and the antagonist distort its objective and its emphasis, thereby making an extended and a reasoned discussion of his examination difficult. His attitude toward his criticisms of orthodox belief was that they were skirmishes or battles in a continuing war for the minds of men; therefore, he did not not intend to participate in restrained debate.

But Ingersoll is not alone in deserving blame for the polemics of the dispute; in fact, some of the blame belongs to his theological opponents, whether of the clergy or not, who not only made even harsher attacks upon him but sometimes indulged in personal attacks upon his motives and integrity, in obscenities, and even in threats and warnings of physical violence. Ingersoll delighted in baiting such opponents, and he deserves consideration for maintaining, under the circumstances, the level that he did.

Nevertheless, in spite of its lapses, "Some Mistakes of Moses" is important in Ingersoll's canon. Not only does it exemplify Ingersoll's ability to examine and reason and to prepare in depth as he usually did in the courtroom but seldom did on the political or lecture platform, but it also provides valuable insight into the nature of biblical critical analysis in those transitional years. A learned layman rather than a scholar, and a trained and skillful attorney, Ingersoll is not interested in the often pedantic, mild, and carefully qualified disputes of the library; he is, instead, interested in indicting, in making and presenting a case for the prosecution to a jury of his peers, and the result is as skillful as his appeals to the jury in the *Star Route* trials. However, no practical means of evaluating effectiveness in an immediate verdict is possible in disputes such as this one; but, in reception in sustained interest, and in contributing to Ingersoll's reputation as America's leading Freethinker, the effectiveness of the lecture was as great as anything he had done.

VIII   *Other Religious Essays*

Other religious lectures of the period—among them "Some Reasons Why" (1881), "The Great Infidels" (1881), "Orthodoxy" (1884), "Which Way" (1884), and "Myth and Miracle" (1885)—raise and repeat most of the issues in these earlier works. "Some Reasons Why" is another exercise in rational biblical criticism, but it is repetitious and decidedly inferior to "Some Mistakes of Moses." Couched in generalities rather than in specific arguments, "Some Reasons Why" is neither polemical nor carefully supported; it is merely doctrinaire. Lacking much of the antagonism of the earlier lecture, it nevertheless emphasizes Ingersoll's agnosticism without ambiguity as he defines the origin of the Bible:

Do not misunderstand me. I insist that every passage in the Bible upholding crime was written by savage man. I insist that if there is a God, he is not, never was, and never will be in favor of slavery, polygamy, wars of extermination, or religious persecution. Does any Christian believe that if the real God were to write a book now, he would uphold the crimes commanded in the Old Testament? Has Jehovah improved? Has infinite wisdom become more merciful? Has infinite wisdom intellectually advanced? (II, 329)

"The Great Infidels" is based upon two factors—first, Ingersoll's interest in his predecessors among nonorthodox thinkers, all of whom he was fond of referring to as infidels and then of demonstrating their great value to mankind; second, the tendency for clergymen to construct mythical deathbed scenes for them in which they repented of their heresies. Ingersoll knew that such would be done to him after his death—as, indeed, it was—and in letters and papers he deliberately denied such a fate in advance. In this lecture, he first defines the nature of religious infidelity and the roles of infidels in human progress—and then he deliberately makes it clear that he is one of them. He examines the pious myths that surround the deaths of six of his infidels: Julian the Apostate, Spinoza, Voltaire, Diderot, David Hume, and Thomas Paine. Each myth, Ingersoll insists, is a fabrication, a slander on the memory of an honest, courageous, and free man. He concludes that each of these men had made far greater contributions to human progress than any of his detractors or calumniators.

The lecture is among Ingersoll's weakest, both because it is poorly organized and because he tries to do too much in too little time. The result is generality without evidence, rhetoric without substance. Had he focused entirely either upon the nature of infidelity or upon the death scenes of his infidels, exploring either in more depth and detail, the results would have been much stronger. However, the lecture was not prepared for publication during Ingersoll's lifetime but reconstructed from notes by his editors; consequently, much of the content and development as it was delivered have undoubtedly been lost. This lecture is one of the many that Ingersoll delivered from notes, but it is one of the few he did not personally rewrite for publication.

IX *Published Confrontations*

In the early 1880's, Ingersoll became involved in one of his muchpublicized, published confrontations with a representative of religious orthodoxy. The reception of "Some Reasons Why" and "The Great Infidels" was so dominated by strong clerical protests that the editor of the *North American Review,* Allen Thorndyke, opened his pages to the controversy; and the ensuing debate continued sporadically throughout the decade beginning in 1881. Ultimately, Ingersoll wrote seven articles for the magazine; and his international array of opponents—Judge Jeremiah S. Black, the Reverend Dr. Henry M. Field, William Ewart Gladstone, and Henry Cardinal Manning—contributed a total of five. Although the results were inconclusive at best, the exchange created the sensation that the editors of the *North American Review* undoubtedly sought.

Ingersoll's first article, "The Christian Religion," appeared in the August, 1881, issue. In it, Ingersoll was far more restrained than in any of his lectures refuting or opposing religious orthodoxy. His arguments are largely those that he had used in the lectures; but the materials, particularly the comparisons between biblical statements and those of other religious bodies, are detailed, rational, and obvious. Only occasionally, as in the following excerpt, does he conclude with loaded rhetoric, and it is mild in comparision with his earlier indictments:

... Jehovah ordered a Jewish general to make war, and gave, among others, this command: "When the Lord thy God shall drive them before thee, thou shalt smite them and utterly destroy them; thou shalt make no covenant with them, nor show mercy unto them." And yet Epictetus ... gave this marvelous rule for the guidance of human conduct: "Live with thy inferiors as thou woulds't have thy superiors live with thee."

... Jehovah, "from the clouds and darkness of Sinai," said to the Jews: "Thou shalt have no others Gods before me ... Thou shalt not bow down thyself to them nor serve them; for I, the Lord thy God, am a jealous God, visiting the iniquities of the fathers upon the children, unto the third and fourth generation of them that hate me." Contrast this with the world put forth by the Hindu into the mouth of Brahma: "I am the same to all mankind. They who honestly serve other gods, involuntarily worship me. I am he who partaketh of all worship, and I am the reward of all worshipers."

Compare these passages. The first, a dungeon where crawl the things begot of jealous slime; the other, great as the domed firmament inlaid with suns. (VI, 12–13)

His conclusions in many ways, even in terminology and structure, parallel those of "Some Reasons Why"; and he ends on a note of certainity that orthodoxy is dead: "The dogmas of the past no longer reach the level of the highest thought, nor satisfy the hunger of the human heart. While dusty faiths, enbalmed and sepulchered in ancient tents, remain the same, the sympathies of men enlarge; the brain no longer kills its young; the happy lips give liberty to honest thoughts; the mental firmament expands and lifts; the broken clouds drift by; the hideous dreams, the foul, misshapen children of the monstrous night, dissolve and fade" (VI, 28).

Judge Black's rebuttal, printed in the same issue, examined, refuted, and denied Ingersoll's allegations point by point. Black—an orthodox Campbellite, a Democrat, and formerly attorney general and secretary of state in James Buchanan's cabinet, and consequently, the target of much indirect Ingersoll invective on all three counts—entered the contest with eagerness but restraint. As his refutations increased in intensity, however, he veered on occasion from his opponent's ideas to his opponent, as when he wrote that Ingersoll was a blasphemer and that "Mr. Ingersoll, as a zealous apostle of 'the gospel of dirt,' must be expected to throw a good deal of mud" (VI, 59). But his article, together with Ingersoll's, illustrates graphically the futility of what inevitably becomes argument rather than debate.

According to the prepublication agreement, each man was to furnish another article; and Ingersoll did so. But Black, insisting that the *Review* had been unfair to him, would not. In his reply to Black, however, Ingersoll, goaded by the personal attack, rose with a vengeance to the attack. He pointed out that Christ was also a blasphemer according to Black's definition; he denied Black's parallels between the wars of Israel and of America; and he made ridiculous Black's assertion that he was a "Christian policeman" attempting to silence disruption. Above all, however, Ingersoll rejoiced in the opportunity to attack Black's feeble attempt to justify the Bible's justification of slavery by insisting that Abolitionist opposition to the institution in America was political and of dubious morality. Combining an attack on Black's Democratic background and his words, Ingersoll made one of his most powerful public personal attacks on a religious opponent:

> According to Mr. Black, there will be slavery in heaven, and fast by the throne of God will be the auction block, and the streets of the New Jerusalem will be adorned with the whipping-post, while the music of the harp will be supplemented by the crack of the driver's whip. If some good Republican would catch Mr. Black, "incorporate him into his family, tame him, teach him to think, and give him a knowledge of the true principles of human liberty and government, he would confer upon him a most beneficent boon." (VI, 70)

Although Ingersoll insists that "I have nothing to do with the character of my opponent. His character throws no light upon the subject, and is to me a matter of perfect indifference" (VI, 74), he makes much use of innuendoes about shortcomings in Black's intelligence, thus giving support to his premise that evil grows out of ignorance. But the bulk of the essay consists of refutations of Black's refutations, as he reminds his readers that "We should remember that ignorance is the mother of credulity . . ." (VI, 109); and he concludes by turning Black's argument about the evils of the French Revolution having surpassed those described in the Bible back on Black: the people of that revolution, he insists, "placed upon a Nation's brow these stars:—Liberty, Fraternity, Equality—grander words than ever issues from Jehovah's lips" (VI, 117).

In the exchange there is no doubt that Ingersoll had the better of his opponent in logic, debate, argument, and invective. Furthermore, because Black had begun the use of personal attack in the exchange, Ingersoll was the recipient of a good deal of popular support; and among his supporters was Walt Whitman, a friend of both Black and Ingersoll, who felt that Black had been too personal. Black, however, refused to reply to Ingersoll's last essay in the *North American Review;* but he finally published a reply in a Philadelphia newspaper that was presumably more sympathetic to his cause.

The exchange with the Reverend Henry M. Field, the owner-editor of the *New York Evangelist* and a liberal Presbyterian, took place in the *North American Review* in 1888. Field, a personal friend of Ingersoll, like William Gladstone, was shocked by Ingersoll's tone in attacking Black and by his rejection of orthodoxy without equivocation. Consequently, in an open letter to Ingersoll, published in the *Review,* Field raised those issues, particularly about the vigor with which Ingersoll had mounted his attack: "I could hardly believe my eyes as I read, so inexpressibly was I shocked. Things which I held sacred you not only rejected with unbelief, but sneered at with contempt. Your words were full of a bitterness so unlike anything I had heard from your lips, that I could not reconcile the two, till I reflected that in Robert Ingersoll (as in the most of us) there were two men, who were not only distinct, but contrary the one to the other—the one gentle and sweet-tempered; the other delighting in war as his native element . . ." (VI, 123).

After this restrained opening that set both the tone and the boundaries for their exchange, Field went on—with courage, restraint, and sincerity—to define the nature of faith rather than to compete on Ingersoll's rational battleground as Black had foolishly done. Science, Field insisted, could take man only part of the way to truth; only faith could take him the full journey.

Ingersoll's reply was equally restrained; Field's letter he said, was "manly, candid and generous," unlike much of the invective he had received. Then he points out the reality and necessity of rational differences among rational, intelligent men—a thought that in itself was a major public concession for Ingersoll although he had often privately expressed the same idea. But, again, in spite of the continued restrained tone, combined with temperate questions, words, and illustrations, the rational questions are posed; and the answers are demanded within the same rational context.

In a second pair of letters in the *Review,* actually, as Field expressed it, simply the adding of a few words to remarkably clear arguments devoid of polemics by both men, both tone and position remained unchanged, just as the issue between them remained unresolved. The exchange following, that between Gladstone and Ingersoll, remained on essentially the same plane: considerably higher in every respect than that between Ingersoll and Black. But the issue remained unresolved, just as it did in the later exchange between Ingersoll and Cardinal Manning. However, Manning, in the dignity of his office, refused to debate; instead he restated, with much detail and documentation, the role of faith as defined by his church. But this position, particularly that which stressed the role of the church fathers in defining that faith, Ingersoll could not accept: "The testimony of the 'Fathers' is without the slightest value. They believed everything—they examined nothing. They received as a waste-basket receives. Whoever accepts their testimony will exclaim with the Cardinal, 'Happily, men are not saved by logic' " (IV, 396).

With the issue apparently closed—although the *North American Review* later sponsored an equally indecisive symposium on divorce that included Ingersoll, Cardinal Gibbons, and Bishop Henry C. Potter—the partisans of each sides were convinced of victory. Thomas Henry Huxley, among others, wrote his congratulations to Ingersoll, together with succinct comments on the nature of the opposition:

> . . . I have not read Manning, and do not mean to. I have had many opportunities of taking his measure—and he is a parlous windbag—and nothing else, absolutely. Gladstone's attack on you is one of the best things he has written. I do not think there is more than 50 per cent more verbiage than necessary, nor any sentence with more than two meanings. If he goes on improving at this rate, he will be an English classic by the time he is ninety. . . .[3]

Ingersoll's reply was equally candid—much more so than his replies to Field, Gladstone, or Manning; and he apparently missed Huxley's irony. This reply unquestionably shows the reason for Ingersoll's unrelenting prosecution of orthodoxy:

> Your estimate of Mr. Gladestone is generous. It does not seem to me that he can live long enough to become a classic.

Your description of the Cardinal is perfect. I was greatly disappointed in both of these men. It is hard to have any respect for an intellect that in this age accepts the orthodox creed.—I feel that the brand of intellectual inferiority is over the theological brain.[4]

X   *Minor Essays of the 1880's*

While the latter part of the exchange was going on, Ingersoll wrote "Orthodoxy," "Which Way," and "Myth and Miracle"—all successful lectures published in 1884 and 1885. Unfortunately, none of the three is a major work, but each in its own way breaks new ground in Ingersoll's continued warfare with theology. In "Orthodoxy," Ingersoll bases his arguments upon a conviction that orthodoxy is dying, that infidelity is growing, and that ultimately the forces of reason will triumph. But the bulk of the lecture is devoted to examining those forces which "have shattered the shield and shivered the lance of superstition": the rise of Islam, the destruction of art, the discovery of America, the rise of science, and the very nature of the orthodox creed. Above all, however, he insists that the heart of orthodoxy's weakness and the source of its ultimate destruction lie in its denial and destruction of human love.

In "Which Way," Ingersoll contrasts man's choices for seeking and finding explanations to the problems that vex him: the natural way, that of reason and logic; and the supernatural way, "by prayer and ceremony to obtain the assistance, the protection of some phantom above the clouds" (III, 399). In it, as in Ingersoll's other similar works, his view of the issues and the logical outcome are clear as the forces of reason and of superstition collide. Virtue, humanity, reason, and love, he says, are the weapons by which superstition, malice, and ignorance are to be overcome. But Ingersoll again replaces evidence with rhetoric, and his conclusion is his climax—a vision of the perfect world of the future:

I look . . . toward the future now. The popes and priests and kings are gone,—the altars and the thrones have mingled with the dust. . . . A new religion sheds its glory on mankind. It is the gospel of this world, the religion of the body, of the heart and brain, the evangel of joy. I see a world at peace. . . . I see a race without disease of flesh or brain, shapely and fair, the married harmony of form and use, and as I look life lengthens, fear dies, joy deepens, love intensifies. The world is free. This shall be. (III, 448—49)

"Myth and Miracle" is a restrained plea for the abandonment of faith in both because "For many ages religion has been tried . . ." but in every instance without success: "In all nations and in all ages, religion has failed. The gods have never interfered. Nature has produced and destroyed without mercy and without hatred. She has cared no more for man than for the leaves of the forest, no more for nations than for hills of ants, nothing for right or wrong, for life or death, for pain or joy . . ." (II, 467).

In thus anticipating the Naturalism of Stephen Crane, Frank Norris, and Theodore Dreiser, a decade and more in the future, Ingersoll defines the post-Darwinian reality—the only reality, he was convinced, that man can know. But, unlike the Naturalists, Ingersoll insisted that there can be more; characteristically, his faith in man's will and reason asserts that "Man through his intelligence must protect himself . . ." (II, 468) and that, if he is willing, he can progress: "If we wish to reform the world we must rely on truth, on fact, on reason. We must teach men that they are good or bad for themselves, that . . . an act is good, bad, or indifferent according to its consequences . . ." (II, 473—74).

Here Ingersoll anticipates another post-Darwinian intellectual movement, that of philosophical pragmatism; and, like John Dewey and William James, he sees in it the means whereby man can not only free himself from the guilt-ridden absolutes of the past but also build a firm superstructure upon a universe in flux and thus find meaning and fulfillment as a social rather than as a spiritual or biological being.

Throughout the rest of the decade of the 1880's, Ingersoll wrote little more except minor works in his continued war against theology and for man. But his testiness against what he considered the arrogance of the religious orthodoxy continued. In 1886, he exhibited that testiness in a typical manner in replying to a Baptist committee which had asked him for financial aid, one of many such requests and inquiries he received:

I hardly know why you saw fit to send "An Appeal" to me. . . . It seems . . . that you had a church—that it had been dedicated to "the Lord God of Israel," as you call him, but afterwards this same Lord God of Israel "tossed your church to the ground," leaving you without any place of worship.

I feel like acquiescing in what the Lord has done. He knows, better than I, whether he wants a Baptist Church; and, in my judgement he has given what might at least be called "an intimation," that a Baptist Church, in that particular locality, was not pleasing in his sight. Why should the "Lord God of Israel" destroy his own property? He is said to "hold the winds in his fists". Why did he open his hand at DeLeon: Is it possible that the "Lord God of Israel" destroys that which he wished to see rebuilt? Maybe he is simply trying your faith. If so, you should not apply to others. You should furnish the evidence yourselves.

My position is this: If the "Lord God of Israel" wants a Bapist Church at DeLeon, let him change the wind, and blow the old one back.[5]

Such an insignificant request, apart from its questionable judgment and taste, hardly seems to warrant either the vindictiveness or the intensity of this attack, but it was undoubtedly an opportunity Ingersoll could not resist. Yet, especially in the light of his well-known kindness, generosity, and willingness to contribute to innumerable causes and persons, some of them questionable, the request seems more acceptable than the reply; for the simplicity of the Baptists of DeLeon, Texas, hardly deserved such an attack on the basis of their simple faith.

In the 1890's, the last decade of Ingersoll's life, he was most prolific in his antitheological writings and lectures, primarily because his law practice had been diverted into civil rather than criminal cases and because his interest in active political campaigning had waned, except in the campaign of 1896. With the proliferation of the dissemination of his views, Ingersoll became even more bluntly aggressive than he had in the past, but in his statements there was little new, although he did explore some of the issues in greater depth than he had in the past.

XI   *"About the Holy Bible" and "The Foundations of Faith"*

In 1894, his major work was "About the Holy Bible," an attempt, he asserted, to tell the truth about the Bible. He had to do so, he said, because preachers, professors, politicans, editors, merchants, and even clerks dared not. Each of them is in a economic and social trap, he said; consequently, he is powerless to point out the evidence it contains within it that refutes its claim to be sacred, to be inspired, and to be a moral guide. Consequently, Ingersoll, determined, as a free man, to tell the truth that others ignore or fear to tell, and he examines it in the light of the humanistic reason that he had employed before. The result contains little that is new, except for expanded specific detail: the ironic inconsistencies and pettiness of the Ten Commandments; the savagery in the Old Testament stories of Achan, Elisha, Daniel, and Joseph; the character of Jehovah; and the inconsistencies among the Gospels in the New Testament. However, Ingersoll adds a new approach: an examination of the philosophy and the character of Christ, both of which he rejects: the first, as foolish; the latter, as ignorant. Here, too, Ingersoll finds evidence for his interpretation of Christ as he examines the nature of his life and his last words.

> All human ties were held in contempt; this world was sacrificed for the next; all human effort was discouraged. God would support and protect.

> At last, in the dusk of death, Christ, finding out that he was mistaken, cried out: "My God! My God! Why has thou forsaken me? " (III, 509)

Ingersoll then concludes: "Why did he go dumbly to his death, leaving the world to misery and to doubt? I will tell you why. He was a man, and did not know" (III, 509).

"The Foundations of Faith," published in 1895, is almost entirely repetitious of his examination of the Bible except that he focuses upon specific portions of Christian faith as they relate to the Bible: the nature of God, the nature of Christ, and the concept of the Trinity. He concludes that "The Old Testament is absurd, ignorant, and cruel,–the New Testament is a mingling of the false and the true. . . ." A simple essay, it is unimportant in the Ingersoll canon. However, Ingersoll followed this with two major essays, "Why I Am An Agnostic" and "How to Reform Mankind," both published in 1896. The former is an intensely personal statement that incorporates within it the sum of his experiences, thoughts, reasoning, and conclusions; the latter is an attempt to provide a blueprint for the man-centered humanistic utopia that he saw in the future.

XII *"Why I Am An Agnostic"*

"Why I Am An Agnostic" contains, first of all, the story of Ingersoll's rejection of the faith that he had inherited, of the conflict between revelation and experience, and of his rejection of the evidence of revelation and the acceptance of that of experience. Copiously illustrated with personal anecdotes designed to make vivid the reality of his experience, it is the most personal of Ingersoll's writings; and Ingersoll creates a valuable social and psychological document as he re-creates the impact of arbitrary Calvinism upon a sensitive, inquisitive boy in the nineteenth century when America was becoming a pluralistic, secular society and the monolithic theocratic society was disappearing. The essay records, too, the growth of indignation at and then hatred of a system that values and even deifies inhumanity, brutality, trickery, and dishonesty. After recounting one particularly vivid re-creation of horror in a revivalist sermon, he remembered that suddenly he was free:

> For the first time I understood the dogma of eternal pain—appreciated "The glad tidings of great joy." For the first time my imagination grasped the height and depth of the Christian horror. Then I said, "It is a lie, and I hate your religion. If it is true, I hate your God."
>
> From that day I have had no fear, no doubt. For me, on that day, the flames of hell were quenched. From that day I have passionately hated every orthodox creed. That Sermon did some good. (IV, 17)

Ingersoll then reviews the books and writers that reinforced his freedom: Burns, Byron, Shelley, Keats, and the supreme revelation, Shakespeare, all of whom contributed to his faith in man; and Paine, Gibbon, Voltaire, and others who confirmed his disbelief. Finally, he concludes by re-creating his sense of freedom:

> When I became convinced that the Universe is natural—that all the ghosts and gods are myths, there entered into my brain, into my soul, into every drop of my blood, the sense, the feeling, the joy of freedom. . . . There was for me no master in all the wide world—not even in infinite space. I was free—free to think, to express my thoughts—free to live to my own ideal—free to live for myself and those I love—free to investigate, to guess and dream and hope. . . . I was free. I stood erect and fearlessly, joyously, faced all worlds. . . . (IV, 65—67)

"Why I Am An Agnostic" is neither an attack nor a polemic but the most intensely personal of all Ingersoll's utterances, it is, at the same time, one of his best. It provides a deep insight into the man behind the polemics, the vindictiveness, the supreme self-confidence, and the great joy in living as well as the paradoxes that constituted Ingersoll's nature. The closest thing to an autobiography that he was ever to write, in many ways it serves as one; and it exhibits a remarkable degree of self-honesty, at least in examining the surface relations of his formative years. Unfortunately, however, it does not recognize a willingness, perhaps even an eagerness, to take refuge in visionary generalities without substance or foundation, as he invariably did when examining the world that his freedom would create.

III   *"How to Reform Mankind"*

Nevertheless, in "How to Reform Mankind" he attempted to point the way and delineate the means of creating that world. Intended to be his definitive statement of humanistic principles, just as "Why I Am An Agnostic" was intended to be the definitive statement of his rejection of orthodoxy, it examines the great social question of the day: the problems of war, of religion, of crime, of housing, of labor, of education, and of motivation. But his solutions are general; they are, in effect, pleas for brotherhood that are based on the beliefs that each man will intuitively come to an understanding of the goodness in himself and in all men and that the world will progress to ultimate perfection. Much as did Emerson in his vision—the youthful Emerson of *Nature*, "An American Scholar," and "The Divinity School Address"—Ingersoll exhibits a faith that is just faith and no more; and the result—in a post-Marxian, post-Darwinian, industrialized and urbanized age—demonstrates little knowledge of an extremely complex society and nothing that approximates a solution.

Instead, Ingersoll concludes with a plea reminiscent of both the orthodox theology that he rejected and the conservative economic policy that he supported:

Let each human being, within the limits of the possible, be self-supporting; let every one take intelligent thought for the morrow; and if a human being supports himself and acquires a surplus, let him use a part of that surplus for the unfortunate; and let each one to the extent of his ability help his fellowmen. Let him do what he can in the circle of his own acquaintance to rescue the fallen, to help those who are trying to help themselves, to give work to the idle. Let him distribute kind words, words of wisdom, of cheerfulness and hope. . . . (IV, 155)

As either statement of belief or plan of action, "How to Reform Mankind" is naive and unsatisfactory, indicating the essential shallowness of his social awareness. But it does demonstrate the sincerity of his convictions; to him, both man and his institutions had the potential for greatness. He was convinced that, once shown the way—essentially in a change of convictions and in an acceptance of humanistic principles—man would become great.

XIV   *Final Agnostic Essays*

The essays and lectures of Ingersoll's last three years—"The Truth" and "A Thanksgiving Sermon" of 1897, "Superstition" of 1898, and

"The Devil" and his final essay, "What Is Religion?" of 1899—are
essentially anticlimactic. Ingersoll had long before developed his major
points in making his reputation and almost all of these writings were
repetitious of them. "The Truth," ostensibly a plea to clergymen to tell
the truth, is in practice a reiteration of his major attacks on orthodoxy,
which he demands that the clergy accept with the same intensity of
faith that he feels. "A Thanksgiving Sermon" refuses thanks for the
abuses of the church and the savagery of orthodoxy, just as it rejects
the idea of thanking God. Instead, it thanks mankind and individual
men for the advances they have made in spite of continued religious
opposition.

"Superstition," ostensibly an examination of the topic in its
broadest implications in the light of reason, reverts to his major
assertion that superstition was, is, and will continue to be the basic of
religion; and he argues that reason is the means for overcoming it. In
"The Devils," he denies that being's existence but insists that belief in
him is at the heart of orthodox religion. He ends with a plea and a
creed. In the plea, he begs for the rejection of the horror incorporated
in the concept of the devil; in the creed, in verse, he declares
independence:

> We have no falsehoods to defend—
>   We want the facts;
> Our force, our thought, we do not spend
>   In vain attacks.
> And we will never meanly try
> To save some fair and pleasing lie. . . .
>
> Is there beyond the silent night
>   An endless day?
> Is death a door that leads to light?
>   We cannot say.
> The tongueless secret locked in fate
> We do not know.—We hope and wait. (IV, 415—19)

Ingersoll's venture into verse—the first for widespread publication,
although he had written poems for private amusement in the past—gives
an unsatisfactorily didactic conclusion, in verse equally weak, to an
argument equally didactic and repetitious. But during these final years
Ingersoll was not concerned with exploring new avenues of thought or
of evidence nor in introducing new, detailed examinations. He was,
instead, carrying on his aggressive warfare with the weapons of wit,

vigor, force, and eloquence that had served him and his causes so effectively, if notoriously, in the past.

Thus his last public lecture, given before the American Free Religious Association in Boston on June 2, 1899, a scant six weeks before he died on July 21, was another lecture in the same vein. "What Is Religion? " was designed for the partisan, favorably disposed audience which heard it. In its brevity, it rejects, again in general terms, the traditional concepts of God, of faith, and of dogmas; and it restates his own: a belief in the reality of material nature, of force, and of human intelligence. "The present," he insists, "is the necessary product of all the past, the necessary cause of all the future." This is all men can know; the rest is speculation and hope. But, although man's reason cannot tell him what is ultimately true, it can tell him what is not; and it can, Ingersoll insists, tell him much about the deterministic nature of the universe.

In general, Ingersoll did little to advance the cause of Freethinking other than through his lecturing and writing. A staunch nonjoiner, he rarely joined forces with others who thought as he did except to repel hostility. Nor did he make major contributions to the body of free thought; and, although he insisted that his guide, his means, and his goal were included in reason, his position was as much the product of faith as the theology he opposed. Yet his importance in the movement toward secularizing America and his role in shifting the direction of man's thinking from the new world to this one must not be underestimated. He made those contributions with force, vigor, wit, and courage; and he expressed them as eloquently as man could possibly do. Determined to free men from the domination of dogma of the past, he made substantial contributions to that cause—and he did so not for the few of libraries and learned journals but for the many across the nation.

CHAPTER 5

"The true transcript of a soul . . ."

ALTHOUGH Ingersoll devoted most of his public life and attention to law, politics, and agnosticism, he devoted a minor but not insignificant amount of it, as well as a substantial part of his private interest, to literature, which, he commented, was, with art and music, that which more nearly reflected the depth and beauty of man's soul. Although he was neither a critic nor a scholar and he had no ambitions or pretensions to be either, he was a sincere if sometimes overenthusiastic appreciator who was eager to share his appreciation with others. In the course of his lifetime, he wrote innumerable letters on the subject; he discussed his favorite writers at every opportunity; and he credited his reading of Shakespeare, Burns, and others with much of what he knew about God and man. But he remained an enthusiastic amateur, an avid worshiper at the shrine of creativity, and a vocal champion, particularly of his favorites. An omnivorous as well as eclectic reader, he ranged widely in his appreciation; and his enthusiasm was as democratic as it was spontaneous.

His major attempts at literary definition and appreciation were rarely critical. Although he brought unformed standards and criteria to his wide reading, he developed standards and criteria of his own. Largely intuitive in nature, they were reflections of his own love and appreciation of language, his passion for finding meaning and potential glory in man's life, and his sense of the dramatic, whether in life or in its re-creation. A man of this world, aware of the pathos, the glory, and the tragedy of man's life, he sought for his favorites those who reflected that paradoxical nature in their work and who rose above it to celebrate life and nature for their own sakes.

I "Robert Burns"

This lifelong enthusiasm of Ingersoll produced major lectures and essays on Robert Burns, William Shakespeare, Walt Whitman, and

Abraham Lincoln, as well as a rich store of references and allusions, much commentary, and a number of minor works. His earliest appreciation, that of Robert Burns, was the subject of a lecture given in 1878, shortly after he and his family had visited Burns's birthplace while touring England in 1878. His estimate of Burns was high then, as it was to remain for the rest of his life; to him, Burns was "possibly the next to the greatest that has ever written in our language. . . ." The greatest, of course, for Ingersoll, was Shakespeare.

Ingersoll examined the background from which Burns had come—the rugged countryside, the lowly family, the limited education, the country slowly struggling to free itself from Calvinism—and then he looked at the essence of his work:

> Robert Burns was a peasant—a ploughman—a poet. Why is it that millions and millions of men and women love this man? He was a Scotchman, and all the tendrils of his heart struck deep in Scotland's soil. . . .
>
> All great poetry has a national flavor. It tastes of the soil. No matter how great it is, how wide, how universal, the flavor of the locality is never lost. Burns made common life beautiful. He idealized the sun-burnt girls who worked in the fields. He put honest labor above titled idleness. He made a cottage far more poetic than a palace. . . . He put native sense about the polish of schools.
>
> . . . We love him because he was a natural democrat, and hated tyranny in every form.
>
> We love him because he was always on the side of the people, feeling the throb of progress. (III, 86—87)

Ingersoll enjoyed Burns and saw in him greatness because he discovered in him the values that he believed in and sought for all men: individualism, native sensibility, uncorrupted innocence, idealization of man, and sentimental awareness of beauty in griminess. Like Ingersoll, Burns made little appeal to the intellect in defining the meaning of a man's life; he made a major appeal to the heart. Moreover, Burns's virtues were Ingersoll's; but Burns observed them more perhaps in their celebration than in their realization, except in the closeness with which he held his family, brothers, and sisters as well as his wife and children. A sentimentalist, Burns appealed to that trait in Ingersoll; and Ingersoll explored him in that light in the lecture, as poet of love, of home, of friendship, of democracy, of personal freedom as opposed to Calvinistic imprisonment. Conveniently ignoring Burns's tendency to be unfaithful and earthy, in his exploration, Ingersoll compares Burns and Tennyson, with startling results that support his major contentions:

> Tennyson was a piece of rare china decorated by the highest art.
>
> Burns was made of honest, human clay, moulded by sympathy and love.
>
> Tennyson dwelt in his fancy, for the most part, with kings and queens, with lords and ladies, with knights and nobles.
>
> Burns lingered by the fireside of the poor and humble, in the thatched cottage of the peasant, with the imprisoned and despised. . . .
>
> Tennyson was touched by place and power, the insignia given by chance. . . .
>
> Burns broadened and ripened with the flight of his few years. . . .
>
> Tennyson was the poet of the past, of the twilight, of the sunset. . . .
>
> Burns was the poet of the dawn, glad that the light was fading from the east. He kept his face toward the sunrise. . . .
>
> Tennyson was what is called religious. He believed in the divinity of decorum, not falling on his face before the Eternal King, but bowing gracefully, as all lords should. . . .
>
> In the religion of Burns, form was nothing, creed was nothing, feeling was everything. He had the religious climate of the soul. . . .
>
> Tennyson was ingenious—Burns ingenuous. One was exclusive, and in his exclusiveness a little disdain. The other pressed the world against his heart. . . .
>
> Men admire Tennyson. Men love Robert Burns. . . . (III, 106—12)

Ingersoll's assessment of Burns is a eulogy rather than an examination, an appreciation rather than an analysis; but with no critical pretensions or ambitions, he did not attempt to use the intellectual tools or standards of the critic. With a taste unformed by education, he found his literary enjoyment in an identity of values and in an identity of spirit with those whose work he enjoyed.

II *"Shakespeare"*

Ingersoll's lecture on "Shakespeare," written in 1891, had been anticipated many times in references over the years; for he often cited the incomparable superiority of Shakespeare's works, in their depth, grasp of reality, visionary humanism, and sheer beauty to the Bible.

Which, he frequently asked, was the truly inspired work? Aware of the continuing debate over the authorship of Shakespeare's works, he determined in 1887 to express his opinion; supported by his logic, he had no doubts:

I am perfectly satisfied that no man with whom the world is acquainted could have been the author of Shakespeare's plays. . . . The world knows Bacon, and I think is satisfied that he could not have been the author of "Lear." For my part, I do not see the slightest evidence in any of his writings that he had sufficient intellect to produce even a good play, or that he had any real dramatic talent. . . .

Now as to the Sonnets. Of course I do not know what reason Mr. O'Connor has for thinking they were written by Sir Walter Raleigh, and I do not wish to know the reason your sixteenth cousin has for saying that they are "poor trash." Some of the finest lines of literature are in the Sonnets. Take, for instance, this one line that has in it all the philosophy of the human heart:

"Love is not love that alters where it
alteration finds."

But as you say, "enough"—because, if Mr. Donnelly has a cipher that demonstrates it, there is no need of wasting arguments, but let me tell you that in my judgement Mr. Donnelly has no cipher, and all that he has written so far, that I have read, is to my mind exactly what your cousin thinks the Sonnets are.

I stand by Shakespeare—the man unspoiled by Oxford—the greatest, the sublimest, of the human race. . . .[1]

Later, Ingersoll stated his opinion in the controversy over Shakespeare's religion:

It has been claimed that Shakespeare was a Catholic—that he was an infidel—and some people have gone so far as to claim that he was a Presbyterian.

The fact is, that Shakespeare could have had no religion. He knew that all religions were subject to change, and consequently he introduced no religious questions into his dramas, knowing that they were simple phases of human thought, or the lack of thought and of emotion. He dealt with the more elemental things—knowing that as long as the race lived, the passions would survive. . . .[2]

Although it is tempting to observe that such foresight would have been remarkable in a popular, crowd-pleasing playwright of Elizabethan

London, it is even more obvious that Ingersoll's certainty, in the light of other, more orthodox certainties, is eloquent testimony to one facet of Shakespeare's genius: his ability to write works so subtly complex that they are subject to such diverse interpretations.

But Ingersoll's certainty about Shakespeare, his work, his worth, and his meaning, which is as innocent of critical objectivity as Ingersoll's view of Burns, is evident in his lecture. Nevertheless, it is flavored with a delightful if unsubtle irony: "More than three centuries ago, the most intellectual of the human race was born. He was not of supernatural origin. At his birth there were no celestial pyrotechnics. His father and mother were both English and both had the cheerful habit of living in this world. The cradle in which he was rocked was canopied by neither myth nor miracle, and in his veins there was no drop of royal blood" (III, 4). His interpretation of Shakespeare's background was, however, of the stuff of myth: his father resisted the Puritans, his mother was "one of the greatest of women," the epitaph on his tomb was to frighten the ignorant people of the countryside. In each case, the interpretation is a certainty; but the certainty is sustained by Ingersoll's faith rather than tangible evidence.

In much of the lecture, Ingersoll refutes those who question Shakespeare's existence or talent as he had earlier in his letters; but the bulk of his emphasis is upon the re-creation of Shakespeare's abilities and upon the superlatives of appreciation; and he couched all he had to say in language much like that he had used in describing Burns. Shakespeare had no identifiable trade or profession, education or training, religious faith or superstition; he was simply a man of genius who, as Ingersoll portrays him, takes on many of the dimensions of the deity that Ingersoll denied:

> . . . He had the observant eyes that really see, the ears that really hear, the brain that retains all pictures, all thoughts, logic as unerring as light, the imagination that supplies defects and builds the perfect from a fragment. . . .
>
> He exceeded all the sons of men in the splendor of his imagination. To him the whole world paid tribute, and nature poured her treasures at his feet. In him all races lived again, and even those to be were pictured in his brain.
>
> He was a man of imagination—that is to say, of genius, and having seen a leaf, and a drop of water, he could construct the forests, the rivers, and the seas—and in his presence all the cataracts would fall and foam, the mists rise, the clouds form and float. (III, 69)

Ingersoll's enthusiasm was as sweeping as his rhetoric, but again his sincerity is unquestionable. For Ingersoll, normally not at a loss for superlatives, the attempt to describe the impact of Shakespeare was difficult—not in the specific aspects of drama, of poetry, of insight—but in the totality of effect. Without question, his experience with Shakespeare was profound, and in the lecture this profundity is re-created with an intensity beyond that with which he asserted either faith or convictions. Shakespeare looms larger than any living human being that Ingersoll ever encountered or tried to describe in his works.

III   *"Liberty in Literature"*

Nevertheless, "Liberty in Literature," delivered in Philadelphia on October 21, 1891, as a testimonial to Walt Whitman, is restrained but at times almost as eulogistic. Ingersoll and Whitman had been friends for years; they had met and corresponded infrequently, but they had often commented about their admiration for each other. Ingersoll, appreciative of Whitman's long cadences, dynamic rhetorical style, and vivid, democratic imagery, had been Whitman's champion for years before they met, perhaps as early as the mid-1860's. Also a close friend of Horace Traubel, Whitman's companion, Ingersoll often kept in contact with Whitman through him; and he helped celebrate Whitman's seventy-fifth birthday at Reisser's Restaurant in Philadelphia.

The occasion of "Liberty in Literature," or "A Testimonial to Walt Whitman," was a gathering five months after Whitman's birthday in Philadelphia's Horticultural Hall to raise funds for Whitman's benefit. Whitman attended the lecture, and he heard Ingersoll eulogize him as a true poet:

At this time [1855] a young man—he to whom this testimonial is given—he upon whose head have fallen the snows of more than seventy winters—this man, born within the sound of the sea, gave to the world a book, "Leaves of Grass." This book was, and is, the true transcript of a soul. The man is unmasked. No drapery of hypocrisy, no pretence, no fear. The book was as original in form as in thought. All customs were forgotten or disregarded, all rules broken—nothing mechanical—no imitation—spontaneous, running and winding like a river, multitudinous in its thoughts as the waves of the sea—nothing mathematical or measured—in everything a touch of chaos; lacking in what is called form, as clouds lack form, but not lacking the splendor of sunrise or the glory of sunset. It was a marvelous collection and aggregation of fragments, hints, suggestions, memories, and prophecies, weeds and flowers, clouds and clods, sights and sounds, emotions and passions, waves, shadows, and constellations. (III, 252—53)

Here Ingersoll's rhetoric—reflecting a rhetoric as rich, as varied, as dynamic as the work he is praising—seems strikingly appropriate. But he does not remain on this level; instead, he examines *Leaves of Grass* in detail, largely according to its reflections of his own convictions, just as he had analyzed Burns and Shakespeare. But he first takes delight in the popular aversion to Whitman's major work in a manner which he could not apply to the others:

His book was received by many with disdain, with horror, with indignation and protest—by the few as a marvelous, almost miraculous, message to the world—full of thought, philosophy, poetry and music.

In the republic of mediocrity genius is dangerous. A great soul appears and fills the world with new and marvelous harmonies. In his words is the old Promethean flame. The heart of nature beats and throbs in his line. The respectable prudes and pedagogues sound the alarm, and cry, or rather screech: "Is this a book for a young person?" (III, 253)

After castigating those prudes at length as ignorant and dishonest, Ingersoll examines the book as it celebrates the religion of the body, individuality, humanity, democracy, philosophy, and ultimately even old age. But, as in his examination of the other poets, he sees in Whitman a reflection of himself. Ingersoll insists that Whitman, in celebrating the body, sees its celebration and gratification as the end of life and poetry rather than, as Whitman made clear, a point of departure from whence an ultimate perception of the whole of man and of man's goodness is possible. In stressing Whitman's praise of individuality, Ingersoll does not see the ultimate unity of man that Whitman envisions beyond that apparently diverse individualism. Democracy to Ingersoll means "a nation of free individuals"; it is not, in the Whitman sense, a spiritual whole based in brotherhood and in the loss of personal identity. In Ingersoll's examination of Whitman as philosopher, he sees Whitman as one who does not know the nature of the ultimate reality—whereas Whitman insists that is is not necessary to know but simply to accept the reflection of God in himself and in all men. He sees Whitman, as a poet of old age, providing hope rather than the serenity with which Whitman invariably comes to grips with the apparent ambiguity of the final years of one's life.

Again Ingersoll emphasizes appreciation rather than critical analysis and celebration rather than comment, and the result is generally unsatisfactory—particularly because he departs frequently from Whitman to refute or castigate his own antipathies. He does, however, provide an interesting insight: that of a contemporary who revered Lincoln, in his brief examination of "When Lilacs Last in the Dooryard Bloom'd." In re-creating the images of the poem as he had experienced them himself, he provides a sense of immediacy almost impossible to recapture with the passage of that contemporaneity, but he rightly concludes that the poem will outlast the moment: "This poem, in memory of 'the sweetest, wisest soul of all our days and lands,' and for whose sake lilac and star and bird entwined, will last as long as the memory of Lincoln" (III, 297).

Ingersoll is just as perceptive as he concludes when he recaptures the dynamism, the life, and the vivid imagery of Whitman's poems:

The world becomes a personal possession, and the oceans, the continents, and constellations belong to you. You are in the center, everything radiates from you, and in your veins beats and throbs the pulse of all life. . . . You are borne on the tides of eager and swift rivers. . . . You traverse gorges dark and dim and climb the scarred and threatened cliffs. . . . You live the lives of those who till the earth. . . . You are in the great cities. . . on the wide plains. . . and you feel the soft grass yielding under your feet. . . . (III, 303)

Perhaps this passage, more than all the others, gives a clue to Ingersoll's affection for literature and for the strong hold that it maintained upon him. His feeling was for words, for sounds, and for rhythm in the works of others as well as his own. The simple bluntness of Burns, the soaring rhetorical power of *Lear,* the dynamic life force of Whitman were the qualities he sought and attained in his own work, and he found and admired them in others. Each of the writers he most admired had a sharp dramatic instinct and an insight into the paradoxical nature of man; but, more than anything else, each was a master of words. Each was a dream and word merchant rather than a philosopher or priest, and in each Ingersoll saw much of himself—often he saw, it is obvious, more than the works actually contain.

IV   *"Abraham Lincoln"*

The same basis of response to literature is evident in others of Ingersoll's preferences and dislikes. In his lecture on Abraham Lincoln, delivered in 1894, he devoted a portion of his attention to Lincoln's rhetoric, commenting that "Probably there are few finer passages in literature than the close of Lincoln's inaugural address: 'I am loth to close. We are not enemies, but friends. We must not be enemies. Though passion may have strained, it must not break, our bonds of affection. The mystic cords of memory stretching from every battlefield and patriotic grave to every loving heart and hearthstone all over this broad land, will swell the chorus of the Union when again touched, as surely they will be, by the better angels of our nature' " (III, 135).

It is unfortunate that Ingersoll chose this passage, but he was undoubtedly unaware that it had been supplied to Lincoln by Secretary of State William H. Seward and then revised and rephrased by Lincoln. It is equally unfortunate that in quoting incorrectly by substituting "loving" for "living" and "patriotic" for "patriot" he damaged the sound and rhythm which Lincoln had so carefully superimposed upon Seward's suggested text.

Other evidences of the same kind of attraction abound. Ingersoll was condescending, if not contemptuous, toward Emerson, perhaps because of his prominence as a lecturer but primarily because he disliked Emerson's philosophy despite the obvious similarities between them. Emerson's doctrine of compensation, he felt, "would be delightful if it had the facts to support it"; [3] he was too self-possessed; and he was quite remarkable for one who was the product of generations of New England clergymen.

James Whitcomb Riley was to him first-rate; comparable to Burns, he was "the sweetest, strongest singer in our country"; [4] George Eliot was a better poet than novelist, and Ouida was "probably the greatest living novelist, man or woman." [5] He disliked Milton, seeing him as hopelessly Puritan: "Milton gave to the Protestant Church the most outrageously materialistic ideas of the Deity. He turned all the angels into soldiers—made heaven a battlefield, put Christ in uniform and described God as a militia general. His works were considered by the Protestants nearly as sacred as the Bible itself, and the imagination of the people was thoroughly polluted by the horrible imagery, the sublime absurdity of the blind Milton.[6]

He also disliked Dante, but he gave him credit for having "the courage, and what might be called the religious democracy, to put a pope in hell . . ." And inevitably but unaccountably, Ingersoll was the admirer of the poetry and novels of his fellow agnostic Edgar Fawcett, in whose brain were "united the beauty of the poet and the subtlety of the logican."

Although Ingersoll was fond of expressing his literary opinions freely in response to questions—many admirers frequently asked his advice in forming personal libraries, for example—he was not perceptive. His tastes were catholic but unformed; and, with his innate distrust of those whom he termed "pedagogues" and of formal education in general, they were uninformed. But to criticize him for what he was not is unjust, although it is tempting to point out the intensity of his patently absurd convictions. But, more than anything else, he was a man of his time, and he was an orator obsessed by rhetoric and a sentimentalist fascinated by sentiment. As a man of his time, he knew what he liked and was free to express it; and, in an untutored America, he was a free, incisive spirit with insight into the meaning and the values of life. To two generations, Ingersoll was living literature; as such, he introduced them to more than his own, just as he demanded that they think. In so doing, he made literature perhaps suspect to many but appealing to at least a few.

CHAPTER 6

"The whole world is a table, we are the balls, and Fate plays the game."

DURING the evening of July 20, 1899, Robert Ingersoll suffered an attack of what was considered acute indigestion, and the next afternoon he was dead. In contrast to the simple, private funeral service, the public reaction to his death was as great and as controversial as the reaction to his most outspoken lectures. Although Charles Guiteau, Garfield's assassin, as well as countless obscure clergymen, had predicted that Ingersoll would die cursing his life and pleading for forgiveness, his passing had been as quiet and peaceful as the memorial service. But rumors circulated asserting the contrary, including one, circulated by a YMCA lecturer, stating that he had taken poison. These rumors multiplied, even after the family attested to the peaceful, noncontroversial, and nonsensational manner of his death.

The Chicago *Tribune* reported "Ingersoll Dies Smiling"; the Charleston *News and Courier* noted that "Robert Ingersoll died yesterday. Perhaps he knows better now." Almost all the commentary on his life at his death is reflected by one or the other of these extremes, although many clergymen were surprisingly not hostile. Letters of condolence poured in from leading citizens by the hundreds. Mark Twain wrote to Mrs. Ingersoll that "Except for my daughter's, I have not grieved for any death as I have grieved for his. His was a great and beautiful spirit, he was a man—all man, from his crown to his footsoles. My reverence for him was deep and genuine. . . ." Others of his friends and admirers insisted that there would never be another like him.

Conversely, his death was a blessing because he could no longer poison men's minds, according to the Reverend A. D. Traveller of Chicago's Methodist City Missions. There was also much comment abut the nature of the torment to which he had been consigned by a just God. Monuments were subscribed and erected, overturned and defaced. The controversy that surrounded his life and death continues almost three quarters of a century after his death, and yet the basis of that controversy has largely been erased by time, by the evolution of religious dogma, and by the growth of a people from simplicity and innocence to sophisticated disregard for faith as a force for good or evil in the world.

The passage of the basis for the controversy about Robert Ingersoll suggests that he, very much a man of his time, would have found it impossible to become either prominent or controversial today for the same reasons. Even while Billy Graham can fill Madison Square Garden with thousands who are seeking something beyond the immediate in which to have faith, countless thousands more are totally indifferent, just as they are to the proselytizing fundamentalist sects that remain. A tolerance suggesting near-indifference permits one to believe or reject as he chooses, and the possibilities of an Ingersoll's attracting crowds to hear him denounce or decry religous orthodoxy is almost inconceivable in such an atmosphere.

Nor, in an age of mass electronic and photographic entertainment, would his oratorical talents make him a major attraction in the cities and towns. Once remote from either entertainment or celebrity, such places are remote no longer; and electronic amplification, tele-prompters, and careful construction of public images have diminished the contemporary value of such talents. America shall never see the like of Robert Ingersoll again because the twentieth century has made much of what gave him fame superfluous and irrelevant. Very much a man of his time, of a simple society and a simple people, he could not survive complexity.

Yet Ingersoll's importance lies in the fact that he did much to make that complexity inevitable, and in that fact lies the basic paradox in the life and career of Robert Ingersoll. He was, more than anything else, a publicizer of issues and a dramatizer of conflicts in the three major aspects of his career: law, politics, and agnosticism. In none of these areas was he an innovator, nor did he make contributions of any significance or permanence to the intellectual or theoretical background of any of the three. In each, his approach and his convictions were similar, stemming from a firm and consistent belief in the nature of liberty. Liberty, to Ingersoll, was a condition in which each man was to be permitted a maximum opportunity for self-growth physically, mentally, morally, economically, and socially—and with a minimum opportunity for interference by social institutions, whether of church or state, and with subjection only to the restriction inherent in the rights of others. At the same time, for Ingersoll, this maximum permissible human liberty must be accompanied by a strong concern for social justice, for human values, and for the needs as well as the rights for others. Most of his public career, in one way or the other, was based upon his attempt to make these ideals real.

In so doing, he was a liberal in the classic nineteenth-century definition of the term as it had resulted from the concepts of natural rights of the eighteenth century and had been transmuted by Thomas Jefferson into a political philosophy and into a personal way of life. But, in accepting those principles, Ingersoll unwittingly made himself the servant of those political and economic forces that denied them in practice while supporting them in theory. As an orator, lecturer, political partisan, and economic conservative who, like Jefferson, had much faith in man's ability to progress, if not to perfect himself and his institutions, he supported the cause of economic and political determinism while mistaking its goals as well as its means for economic and political progress. Thus, he lent his support to those who abused democratic government in the *Star Route* cases; he justified political ends by using the "bloody shirt" as a means to attain them; and he aided the growth of great concentrations of power and wealth by supporting the protective tariff and the gold standard at the expense of those who were relegated to the lower strata of the economic and political structure.

However, if these were all of Ingersoll's contributions to the evolution of American society in the nineteenth century, his role would be worth little more than a historical footnote. But his attacks on religious orthodoxy had social and economic repercussions far more significant than Ingersoll intended them to have. In teaching men to question the dogmas of religious faith, he taught them to question other dogmas also—among them, the social and economic structure that he supported. In an age dominated by those who supported and lived by the gospel of wealth—an economic faith compounded out of the Protestant ethic, the residue of Puritanism, the pronouncements of Adam Smith and Alexander Hamilton, and the biological determinism of Charles Darwin—he taught men to question a substantial portion of the rationale behind the rise of nineteenth-century American capitalism, just as he taught them to question anything that purported to be a gospel to be accepted on faith and distorted fact rather than on evidence supported by reason.

Thus, although Ingersoll found much support from Andrew Carnegie, one of those who contributed most to the new industrialism and the gospel that supported it, he also found much from Eugene

Debs, who had seen its flaws and who devoted himself to destroying the gospel so that the power and wealth of the new system might be more democratically distributed. At the same time, Ingersoll found himself close personally to and accepted philosophically both by Walt Whitman, an apostle of progress to the end, and by Mark Twain as he denounced man's nature and institutions in his last and most bitter years. His impact on religious thinking was slight in comparison to that of Henry Ward Beecher, who pointed the way toward modernism and the social gospel within the framework of Christianity, but he quickly became a prophet to those who saw beyond the economic, political, and social power structure of the moment.

Ingersoll's emphasis, however ill-defined and abstract, upon human values rather than upon material values was particularly important in making possible the age of progressive reform that was just beginning to be felt in the last years of his life. Clarence Darrow, who was to do much to humanize jurisprudence, found inspiration in Ingersoll, as did John Peter Altgeld in his pardon of those convicted in the Haymarket deaths. His support of Henry George and the Single Tax gave inspiration to Tom L. Johnson and Brand Whitlock in civic reform, both of whom supported the same ends of dignified, secure home ownership for workmen. And finally, in Ingersoll's last years, although he still supported the protective tariff as advantageous for American workmen and for industrial progress, he turned upon the industrialists who "as a clan are so mean and cruel that I hate to advocate anything they are for" and who profited tremendously by the lack of effective competition from abroad.

Yet, perhaps more paradoxical than any other aspect of Ingersoll's life is the fact that he had so little insight into the nature of his epoch, particularly in the rapidly accelerating rate of evolutionary change in almost every conceivable area, especially the intellectual. A strong supporter of "education" in the abstract, he opposed its institutions, while neither seeing nor supporting the movements that led to its secularization and democratization in his own lifetime. A strong supporter of civil rights, particularly for Negroes, he did not make the emergence of Jim Crow and segregation, for which his party bore much responsibility, a political issue as he might have done. An advocate of the rights of women and children, he played no part in the political drive to make those rights realities. A man with strong literary interests, he seemed to be unaware of the attempts of Henry James and William Dean Howells to construct a new Realistic ethic and of Stephen Crane and others to incorporate the new industrialism and post-Darwinian science into a Naturalistic literary philosophy. Actually, Ingersoll—a man whose ideas and values had been formed in the simple society of pre-Civil War America—became prominent and influential in a much more complex society in which he continued to apply the values of the past because he interpreted the events of that complex society in terms of the simple society he understood.

At Ingersoll's death, it was obvious to many of his friends that America would never see his like again because to them he represented the virtues and the values of his age: eloquence, in an age that demanded that talent of those who would be heard; patriotism, at a time when it was valued for its own sake; individualism, when Americans still insisted that man rather than institutions was important and when each man took pride in establishing his own identity; courage, when men admired those who chose not to conform at whatever price necessary; loyalty, when that value was given to men and ideas rather than institutions; hospitality, when men were accepted for what they were rather than what they believed or what they appeared to be to others. These were the qualities that Ingersoll's contemporaries—many ideological foes as well as supporters—saw in him then; and they remain the outstanding qualities that permeate his works and his thinking.

Nevertheless, the vital spirit that gave these qualities their force as well as their being ceased with Ingersoll's death, and the passage of time in a rapidly changing society has made his ideas and his writing of little relevance today. Very much a man of America's past, he has been relegated to little more than a footnote in American history; and perhaps, with his minimal original contributions to American thinking and writing, he merits no more than that footnote.

But, in another sense, he is relevant today; and his presence in its paradoxical simplicity can still be felt, as eloquently and controversially as in his years of public discourse. His relevance and his presence can be felt in his works, the means whereby he made his not insignificant contributions to the course of American events and development. In his works the courage, the eloquence, and the rhetorical magic are as evident as the ideas that even three-quarters of a century later can still evoke the fear, the indignation, and the equally uncritical acceptance that he evoked in person during his lifetime.

Although Ingersoll's powerful presence is no longer able to give them life, the words, the images, the relentless questioning, and the skillfully directed emotion combine to give them a relevance even after most of the issues have long ago been resolved. More important, they point out that the major issue, that of man's origin and purpose, is no closer to resolution; and the major explanations are no more verified or verifiable than in Ingersoll's day. Yet his eloquence, his courage, and his determination have perhaps brought that controversy closer to its ultimate resolution. If they have, his role in the final assessment of man's search for his meaning may take on major proportions, and his place in the history of man's realization of his meaning may be more significant than it seems to be at the moment.

But whether that eventuality comes to pass or not is unimportant. In his works, Ingersoll can still evoke controversy, bring alive a past that was vital and important, shed light on the events and people that made America what it is, and revive his own large personality as it played its significant part. All this capability combines to produce a contribution larger than that of the history of the Presidency in his time. This literary contribution, historical contribution, and social contribution can be ascribed to few others, and Robert Ingersoll is deserving of much more than the obscurity to which he has been relegated.

Notes and References

Chapter One

1. All factual biographical information, unless otherwise cited, comes from C. H. Cramer, *Royal Bob: The Life of Robert G. Ingersoll* (Indianapolis, 1952); Eva Ingersoll Wakefield, Biographical Introduction to *The Letters of Robert G. Ingersoll* (New York, 1951); and biographical essays and letters by Robert Ingersoll. For the interpretation of those facts, I am responsible.

2. Robert G. Ingersoll, *The Works of Robert G. Ingersoll.* With a publisher's preface by C. P. Farrell (New York, 1907), I, 377–79. Hereafter, all volume and page references for quotations from *The Works of Robert G. Ingersoll* will appear in the text of the study.

3. The Chicago *Tribune,* July 22, 1899, quoted in C. H. Cramer, *Royal Bob,* 26.

4. Quoted in *ibid.,* p. 42.

Chapter Two

1. Robert G. Ingersoll, *The Letters of Robert G. Ingersoll* (New York, 1952), 107. Hereafter referred to as Ingersoll, *Letters.*

2. *Ibid.,* 110.

3. The New York *Sun,* June 15, 1883, quoted in Ingersoll, *The Works of Robert G. Ingersoll,* X, 531. Hereafter referred to as Ingersoll, *Works.*

4. Ingersoll, *Letters,* 176.

5. Butte (Montana) *Anaconda Standard,* September 5, 1891, quoted in Ingersoll, *Works,* X, 535.

Chapter Three

1. Indianapolis *Journal,* September 23, 1868, quoted in Ingersoll, *Works,* IX, 21.

2. Ingersoll, *Letters,* 137.
3. *Ibid.,* 143–44.
4. *Ibid.,* 159.
5. *Ibid.,* 160.
6. Chicago *Tribune,* June 16, 1876, quoted in Ingersoll, *Works,* IX, 56.
7. Ingersoll, *Letters,* 162.
8. *Ibid.,* 163.
9. *Ibid.,* 172.
10. *Ibid.,* 181–82.
11. Chicago *Inter-Ocean,* October 9, 1896, quoted in Ingersoll, *Works,* IX, 535–36.
12. Ingersoll, *Letters,* 218.

Chapter Four

1. Ingersoll, *Letters,* 158.
2. Henry Ward Beecher in *The Christian Union,* May 15, 1872, quoted in Ingersoll, *Letters,* 95.
3. Ingersoll, *Letters,* 310.
4. *Ibid.,* 311.
5. *Ibid.,* 272–73.

Chapter Five

1. Ingersoll, *Letters,* 366–67.
2. *Ibid.,* 368.
3. *Ibid.,* 405.
4. *Ibid.*
5. *Ibid.,* 404.
6. *Ibid.*

Selected Bibliography

PRIMARY SOURCES

1. The Works of Robert Ingersoll:

The Works of Robert G. Ingersoll. With a publisher's preface by C. [linton] P. Farrell. 12 Vols. New York: The Dresden Publishing Co., 1907.

The Letters of Robert G. Ingersoll. Edited with a biographical introduction by Eva Ingersoll Wakefield. New York: Philosophical Library, 1951.

2. Collections of Manuscripts:

The Robert G. Ingersoll Papers, Library of Congress.
The Robert G. Ingersoll Papers, Illinois State Historical Library.
The Robert G. Ingersoll Papers, New York Public Library.

SECONDARY SOURCES

1. Bibliography

STEIN, GORDON. *Robert G. Ingersoll—a Checklist.* Kent, Ohio—the Kent University Press, 1969. The first attempt to compile an exhaustive Ingersoll bibliography.

2. Books

AVERY, LILLIAN D. *A Genealogy of the Ingersoll Family in America, 1629–1925.* New York: Frederick H. Hitchcock, 1926. Traces Ingersoll's ancestry.

BAKER, I. NEWTON. *An Intimate View of Robert G. Ingersoll.* New York: C. P. Farrell, 1920. A biographical memoir.

BRADEN, CLARK. *Ingersoll Unmasked; A Scathing and Fearless Exposé of His Life and Real Character.* New York: Clark Braden, 1901. Typical, near-libelous attack.

BRIGANCE, WILLIAM N., ed. *A History and Criticism of American Public Address.* New York: McGraw-Hill, 1943. Revealing comments on Ingersoll's oratory.

COMMAGER, HENRY S. *The American Mind—An Interpretation of American Thought and Character Since the 1880's.* New Haven: Yale University Press, 1950. Discusses Ingersoll in the context of his times.

CRAMER, C. [larence] H. *Royal Bob.* Indianapolis: Bobbs-Merrill, 1952. Good if somewhat apologetic biography.

CURTI, MERLE. *The Growth of American Thought.* New York: Harper & Brothers, 1943. Discusses Ingersoll's place in the evolution of ideas.

CURTIS, FRANCIS. *The Republican Party, 1854–1904.* New York: Putnam's, 1904. Discusses Ingersoll as national political figure.

DARROW, CLARENCE and WALLACE RICE. *Infidels and Heretics.* Boston: The Stratford Co., 1929. Discusses Ingersoll in the light of other unorthodox thinkers.

DUGANNE, A. J. H. *Injuresoal: A Satire for Science.* New York: American Book-Print Co., 1884. Inept but typical satirical attack and warning.

GORHAM, CHARLES T. *Robert G. Ingersoll.* London: C. A. Watts, 1921. Somewhat apologetic biography.

HOFSTADTER, RICHARD. *Social Darwinism in American Thought, 1860–1915.* Philadelphia: University of Pennsylvania Press, 1945. Defines the background of Ingersoll's humanism.

HORNER, CHARLES F. *The Life of James Redpath.* New York: Barse & Hopkins, 1926. Ingersoll's relations with his lecture manager.

HUBBARD, ELBERT. *Little Journeys to the Homes of Great Americans: Robert G. Ingersoll.* East Aurora, New York: The Roycrofters, 1911. The Ingersoll home and memories.

KITTREDGE, HERMAN E. *Ingersoll, A Biographical Appreciation.* New York: Dresden Publishing Co., 1911. Biographical apology and defense.

LAMPERT, REV. L. [OUIS] A. *Notes on Ingersoll.* Buffalo: Buffalo Catholic Publication Co., 1884. Theological refutation of Ingersoll's arguments.

LEWIS, JOSEPH. *Ingersoll The Magnificent.* New York: The Freethought Press Association, 1957. Biographical eulogy with excerpts from Ingersoll's works.

McCLURE, J. B. ed. *Mistakes of Ingersoll and His Answers Complete.* Chicago: Rhodes & McClure, 1882. Early condemnation.

MUZZEY, DAVID S. *James G. Blaine, A Political Idol of Other Days.* New York: Dodd, Mead, 1934. Traces the relationship with Ingersoll.

PERSONS, STOW. *Free Religion, An American Faith.* New Haven: Yale University Press, 1947. Defines the Freethought tradition.

ROBERTSON, J. M. *A History of Freethought in the Nineteenth Century.* 2 vols. New York: Putnam's, 1930. Cites Ingersoll's role in the movement.

ROGERS, CAMERON. *Colonel Bob Ingersoll.* New York: Doubleday, Page & Co., 1927. A friendly biography.

SMITH, EDWARD G. *The Life & Reminiscences of Robert Green Ingersoll.* New York: National Weekly Publishing Co., 1904. A popularized memoir.

TRAUBEL, HORACE. *With Walt Whitman in Camden.* 3 vols. Boston: Small, Maynard, 1906. Comments on Ingersoll's friendship with Whitman.

WARREN, SIDNEY. *American Freethought, 1860–1914.* New York: Columbia University Press, 1943. Traces Ingersoll's role and influence.

Index